TEACHERS ON INDIVIDUAL-IZATION: THE WAY WE DO IT

Edited by
David A. Shiman
Carmen M. Culver
Ann Lieberman

Foreword by
Samuel G. Sava
Executive Director |I|D|E|A|

A CHARLES F. KETTERING FOUNDATION PROGRAM

McGRAW-HILL BOOK COMPANY
New York   St. Louis   San Francisco   Düsseldorf
London   Mexico   Sydney   Toronto

Library of Congress Cataloging in Publication Data
Main entry under title:

Teachers on individualization.
    (|I|D|E|A| reports on schooling. Early schooling
series) (Series on educational change)
    Bibliography: p.
    1. Individualized instruction—Addresses, essays,
lectures.   I. Shiman, David A., ed.   II. Culver,
Carmen M., ed.   III. Lieberman, Ann, ed.   IV. Series:
Institute for Development of Educational Activities.
Early schooling series.   V. Series: Institute for
Development of Educational Activities. Series on educa-
tional change.
LB1031.T42   372.1'39'4   73-17203
ISBN 0-07-056895-2

|I|D|E|A| is the service mark for the Institute for Development of Educational Activities, Inc., an incorporated affiliate of the Charles F. Kettering Foundation.

|I|D|E|A| was established in 1965 to encourage constructive change in elementary and secondary schools. It serves as the primary operant for the Foundation's missions and programs in education.

As an institution committed to stimulating constructive changes for the benefit of mankind, the Kettering Foundation believes strongly in the potential of education to help bring about such changes.

Robert G. Chollar

President and
Chief Executive Officer
Charles F. Kettering Foundation

CONTENTS

FOREWORD

This volume is part of a series reporting on the five-year Study of Educational Change and School Improvement conducted by the Research Division of the Institute for Development of Educational Activities, Inc. (|I|D|E|A|). |I|D|E|A| was established by the Charles F. Kettering Foundation in 1965 as its educational affiliate and given the specific mission of accelerating the pace of change in education. Before advocating yet another collection of "innovations" based on the best insights then available, we decided to begin by examining the total context in which change was to take place. Under the direction of Dr. John I. Goodlad, |I|D|E|A|'s Research Division selected eighteen schools from eighteen Southern California districts, the "League of Cooperating Schools," to participate in the design and testing of a new strategy for educational improvement. The several volumes now being published by McGraw-Hill report on the variety of human and organizational influences that operated within this new social system of schools.

It would be both premature and pointless to highlight here the basic findings of this study. Each finding must be put in context before its significance can be appreciated. Suffice it to say that while those responsible for a school must have the desire to change before they can do so, desire is not enough. They must also understand what Dr. Goodlad calls "the ecology of change," the complex of factors that can defeat a school staff's most conscientious efforts to improve.

Goodlad and his staff did not try to implement specific innovations. Rather, they sought to develop in the League schools processes of dialogue, decision making, action, and evaluation (DDAE) through which school staffs would become increasingly responsive to school problems and the array of possible solutions to them. The principal and teachers of each participating school sought to become proficient in the DDAE cycle. Over time, a kind of self-renewing ability developed. The schools of the League tried a variety of solutions to their problems, exchanging experiences with one another, learning by seeking help from and teaching one another. The entire process was reinforced through membership in the League.

Most of the schools became interested in improving the quality of learning for each individual student. Teachers read a great deal and turned to such activities as developing learning resource centers, substituting multimedia sets of materials for textbooks, nongrading, and team teaching. To repeat, they did not set out to install innovations. They sought improved solutions to problems identified through the process of DDAE. Frequently, their solutions were innovative in character. Then they shared their successes and failures with other schools in the League.

This volume reports the experiences of teachers who used the resources of the League in improving their individualization of teaching and learning. Other volumes in this series concentrate on the design of the central study, the strategies employed, and the findings gleaned from research data. This volume has no such ambitious goals. We simply think that what these teachers have to say might be helpful to other teachers seeking to improve the quality of individual pupil learning.

The Study of Educational Change and School Improvement provided much of the strategy for the |I|D|E|A| Change Program for Individually Guided Education (IGE) now being used in several hundred schools. It spawned major studies of the change process in schools and nearly forty doctoral dissertations related to these studies. The activities reported here suggest how at least some of the teachers were influenced. On behalf of |I|D|E|A| and the Charles F. Kettering Foundation, I wish to express gratitude to the school board members, administrators, teachers, children, and parents who made all this possible.

Samuel G. Sava
Executive Director
|I|D|E|A|

TEACHERS ON INDIVIDUALIZATION:
THE WAY WE DO IT

INTRODUCTION

David A. Shiman, Carmen M. Culver, and Ann Lieberman[1]

The authors of this book are elementary school teachers who participated in the League of Cooperating Schools. The League was an association between eighteen elementary schools in Southern California
and the Research Division of the Institute for Development of Educa-
tional Activities, Inc. (|I|D|E|A|), an affiliate of the Charles F. Kettering
Foundation. *Teachers on Individualization* is a natural outgrowth of
this association, for one of its goals was to encourage teachers to provide assistance and encouragement to their peers in their efforts to
improve their schools.

The League of Cooperating Schools was established as part of the
five-year Study of Educational Change and School Improvement which
was conducted by the |I|D|E|A| Research Division under the direction
of John I. Goodlad.[2] The project grew out of the observation that after
repeated attempts and various approaches to get schools to change
and adopt recommended innovations, the educational scene today is
pretty much what it was ten or more years ago. What goes on in a
classroom and in the interactions between teacher and child has been
little affected by extensive research into the psychology of learning,
while the physical organization of the school and its division into age-
graded, self-contained classrooms still reflects the old belief that all
children learn at the same rate and in the same manner. Why have
educational research in general and planned interventions into schools
in particular had so little impact?

The Study of Educational Change was an attempt both to introduce change into schools and to study the process by which change
takes place. The first step was to develop an intervention strategy
which would not have the major drawbacks that had flawed other attempts. For example, one model for intervention calls for an outside
expert to go to the school and tell it what to do. However, there are
three objections to this strategy. First, since the expert has been the
source of all wisdom, processes are seldom developed in the school

which will maintain the innovation after the expert has left. Second, the expert, as an outsider, is often viewed by the school staff as an "ivory-tower" educator who does not really understand what it is like to be in a classroom day after day—in other words, his advice is seen as not always relevant to the real-life situation. Third, even if this intervention strategy were highly effective in introducing change in schools, there will never be a sufficient number of experts available to all the schools which need their help.

Another model for intervention calls for packaging the knowledge of experts and presenting it to the schools as a program—for example, for reading or mathematics. These programs certainly could be produced in sufficient numbers to reach all schools who want them. However, a major drawback here is that because the programs are prepackaged, they cannot take into account the circumstances in a given school. Their advice, too, may not be relevant to the situation.

One belief guiding the Study of Educational Change was that the faculties of individual schools know best what needs to be done in their own situation. Therefore, they should decide where, when, and how innovations should be introduced. A major corollary of this belief is that within any group of schools there exists a number of individuals who have faced the problems of schooling and have come up with innovative and workable solutions. These teachers and administrators can provide help and advice to others who are facing the same problems. In addition, by bringing together teachers and administrators from a number of schools, not only will the possible sources of help be multiplied, but each school and teacher can derive support and encouragement for its efforts from the others. Thus, a major component of the strategy was the establishment of the League of Cooperating Schools. Not only would the League schools provide "expert" help for each other, but they would encourage each other to change, be innovative, and be a buffer against the pointing fingers of those who were staying the same.

One problem confronting the project's directors was that of deciding to what extent specific innovations should be endorsed for implementation in the League schools. It was reaffirmed very early in the life of the project that each school did indeed know best what needed doing in its situation, but it also became clear that information had to be made available to school staffs so that they would know the alternatives and options open to them. Individualization of instruction appeared to be a common concern of most schools, and so the |I|D|E|A| Research Division provided a wide array of materials in all forms, including books, pamphlets, reprints of journal articles, microfiche documents, films, speakers, and bibliographies (an example of the bibliographies prepared for the League is the extensive "Selected Bibliography on Individualizing Instruction" by Lillian K. Drag which is included in this volume). However, although the project staff did try to provide a wealth of information to help teachers individualize, it consistently refused to go into the classroom and individualize for teachers or, indeed, to implement any other contemplated innovations. As Jane O'Loughlin points out in her chapter of this book, "Our staff spent a year listening to experts who gave us no answers. How wise they were! They made us find our own way."

In finding their own way, teachers also came up with ideas and practical solutions that no outside expert can provide. And then they became "experts" for each other. Throughout the five-year duration of the project, teachers and administrators from all the League schools were brought together to talk to each other and listen to each other about what they were doing. They were also encouraged to visit other schools in the League and to observe what was being tried, what worked, and what failed in their programs. In addition, they exchanged ideas through the mail and by telephone, organized and participated in conferences and workshops, gave demonstrations of various techniques for individualization, and contributed to a newsletter developed by all the League schools. Teachers provided help for other teachers who were trying to individualize, were teaming for the first time, or were nongrading their classrooms. Their advice was usually practical and down to earth—here's what I do, why don't you try this, and I tried that but it didn't work. *Teachers on Individualization* represents the substance of what went on in those dialogues.

The book grew out of a desire to extend the boundaries of communication beyond the eighteen League schools. It differs from many other books on the same theme in that it is written for teachers by other teachers who are actually in the classroom. It is written for those new teachers fresh from teacher training programs, bubbling with ideas and enthusiasm but lacking some basic organizational and technical skills. And it is written for experienced teachers who are frustrated with what they are doing and eager though hesitant to change. Finally, it is written with the hope that almost any teacher will be able to find among the divergent philosophies, teaching techniques, and organizational styles presented here an approach to individualizing instruction with which he feels comfortable.

In early discussions about this book, the teachers became acutely aware of the difficulty of arriving at a definition of individualized instruction. Some teachers defined individualization in terms of rate or pace of learning; others contended that it is achieved through the differentiation of curriculum offerings at different times of the day or week. For some, individualization meant providing students with a variety of choices in activities to move them toward some common goal. Others focused on the importance of having students themselves choose objectives and follow through, irrespective of any teacher-defined goal.

But the fact that considerable diversity in philosophy and approach to individualization is offered in this book should by no means suggest that the search for a meaningful definition has not been guided by certain values. On the contrary: All those who contributed to *Teachers on Individualization* share the belief that individualization must have as its ultimate goal the possibility that each child can become a self-directed learner. The teacher must recognize, appreciate, and promote the uniqueness of the individual child if each child is to develop a favorable view of himself and a greater awareness of his capabilities. To achieve these ends, the teacher must do more than just love the child. Instructional plans must include the gathering of data about the child's development and learning and the use of such data as a guide, so that the teacher can effectively help him grow.

One other crucial point needs to be made concerning the values which the writers bring to this book. They feel that no definition of individualization in a school setting can be complete without a recognition of the fact that children can and should learn from each other. Group experiences, whether they be discussion sessions, collaborative projects, or merely shared activities, need to be incorporated into the classroom program. The school is a social institution, and the individual child needs to learn and develop within a social context.

So much has already been written about the physiological, psychological, emotional, and intellectual differences that exist among individuals that it needs no reiteration here.[3] Suffice it to say that the research conducted into differential rates of learning and maturation mandates some sort of diversification in our instructional strategies.

We know that each human being is unique, possessed of his own strengths and weaknesses, his own interests, and his own capabilities and potentialities. To deny this fact is not only to fly in the face of conclusive research findings but also to close our eyes to the individual's possibilities.

Because the writers of this book are united in their belief in the value of individualized instruction, the reader will find throughout the chapters very little attempt to justify it. Instead, each writer concentrates her (or, in one case, his) efforts on explaining and describing, in as much detail as possible, her own program for individualization. Each chapter begins with some introductory remarks in which the writer sets the stage, traces her own development as a teacher, and shares her own attitudes. This is important, for it is not possible to explain one's approach to teaching merely by "telling what you do." The way each person teaches is an expression of his professional growth experiences, his values, and philosophy. The individual teacher is not a static human being performing certain acts at a particular juncture in time. Each is part of a process, for each has grown, has questioned the assumptions on which his own actions are based, and has changed.

After these introductory remarks, each writer launches into a discussion of her approach. She explains how she initiates her program, how she maintains and monitors it to insure that each child is learning, and how she evaluates it. These descriptions extend beyond merely discussing how to organize, how to teach, and how to interact. Implementing an individualized program involves coping with problems of time and space usage and decision-making procedures, changing teacher and student roles and curriculum orientation, as well as the tasks of diagnosis, prescription, and evaluation. Each is part of an integrated process, and changes in one area frequently promote or necessitate changes in others.

The reader should keep several points in mind while reading and using this book. First, the writers no doubt will leave many questions unanswered. Even though such basic items as samples of learning contracts, floor plans, letters to parents, and record-keeping systems are supplied, some readers will certainly contend that much has been left unsaid. This is true. The writers cannot and would not, even if they could, provide a step-by-step, day-by-day blueprint for individualization. This, in itself, would be contrary to the spirit of individualized learning—for teachers are individuals, too—and would be far more prescriptive than any of them would be comfortable with. Because each class is different, and each teacher is different, all that can be offered is an aid, and perhaps a guide, to help teachers move in a new direction.

Second, the reader should not be disappointed by the fact that his particular type of classroom situation is not described. Some of the writers team teach in nongraded, open classrooms. Others are by themselves in self-contained, single-grade situations. But much of what has been written has applications far broader and more diverse than the specific situation described by any particular author. Certainly many teaching and organizational techniques developed in team teaching situations are adaptable for use by the single teacher. Third, the reader will find that most of the writers have described their programs in the language arts (reading and spelling) in greater detail, dealing with other subject areas such as math or social studies only tangentially. This fact does not preclude the possibility that the techniques described can be transferred to other subject areas. One's approach to the teaching–learning situation is not generally dictated by the subject matter content but by the teacher's view of how learning takes place.

Finally, in the spirit in which this book is offered, we hope it will result in the creation of lines of communication between those who read it and those who wrote it. You are invited to share your ideas with the authors, criticize what they have written, and make suggestions for improvement. It is through this type of dialogue that one grows and learns as a teacher. The Research Division of |I|D|E|A| will be happy to serve as a clearinghouse for any such communications.

NOTES

1   As |I|D|E|A| staff members involved with the League of Cooperating Schools, we worked to help teachers realize how much they had to contribute to each other, to make them aware that, as the practitioners who were struggling to change their own approach to teaching and to provide the best possible learning experience for each of their students, they had a wealth of knowledge to share. Further information concerning the history of the League and the peer group strategy on which it was based may be found in the other books in the |I|D|E|A| series (McGraw-Hill) and the several films on the project developed by and available from |I|D|E|A|.

2   The story of the project and its findings is discussed in Mary M. Bentzen and Associates, *Changing Schools: The Magic Feather Principle,* McGraw-Hill, New York, in press.

3   See Robert M. Gagné (ed.), *Learning and Individual Differences,* A Symposium of the Learning Research and Development Center, University of Pittsburgh, Charles E. Merrill Books, Columbus, Ohio, 1967; Thomas R. Murray and Shirley M. Thomas, *Individual Differences in the Classroom,* David McKay Co., New York, 1965; Association for Supervision and Curriculum Development, *Human Variability and Learning: Papers and Reports,* Fifth Curriculum Research Institute, ed. by Walter B. Waetjen, The Association, a department of the National Education Association, Washington, D.C., 1961; as well as the comprehensive bibliography provided in this volume.

CHAPTER 1

NOTES TO A NEW TEACHER

Sally Huffman

This chapter opens a window on the thoughts of a teacher as she muses about all the great things every teacher would like to accomplish, as well as the nagging doubts that accompany these great highs.

The chapter traces a favorite year of working with fourth, fifth, and sixth graders, many of whom suffered grave feelings of "defeat," "poor self-images," and "poor peer relationships." Learning became personalized, self-motivated, and, for most of the children, their first successful school experience.

So you are a new teacher. *Great.* You have high hopes of individualizing a classroom. *Great.* It is assumed that you are an individual yourself. Another *great.* Now where do you go? You look at yourself, who you are, how you feel about yourself, how you feel about teachers, teaching, and children. You think back to when you were a child and what teachers did to you and what you did to teachers. You look at the college or university you attended, the courses you took, and the reactions you had to those courses. You try to recall the many times you have had a reaction to what the great and not so great educators have said to you in books and what you do and don't agree with. Then again, you remember that you are you, an individual, no one else like you, just your own little snowflake or your own little thumbprint; and you are meeting people, including children, all the time, and they also are their own little snowflake or thumbprint, and you take a great oath that you will remember this. If you think deeply about this you will be aware of your great responsibility to children.

It is assumed that the teacher will make the child learn. This is untrue. The old saying "I can't teach you anything" must have come from a wise philosopher. Without the will to learn, learning will not occur. Therefore we teachers do not teach; we merely motivate to learn—a high-class selling job at that. So let us be directors, educators, facilitators, inputters. As facilitators, we get the right stuff into the hands of the right children at the right time. And this takes awareness. So if you don't have it, start developing it. It will be your greatest tool. Once you have awareness, don't assume that it will always be there; it gets rusty, stale, and sometimes dies away. Give it a thousand-mile check now and then, replace worn parts, change the oil, put some new ideas in your carburetor, give it a road test. Sometimes it's just as well to throw the car out and start all over again. (And this applies to those closets full of things forgotten from years past.)

GETTING IT TOGETHER

Because you are an educator it is assumed that you will give that extra measure of time to get yourself and your room into some acceptable state before the first day of school when those scared, rumor-filled, expectant children come to their new room. They too have a grapevine and the word is out on you if you've taught at this school before. If you haven't taught here before they will be watching, evaluating, and placing you in focus. As an adult you will have to be the braver of the two. You will have to have something to tell them. Upon this talk will depend the direction of your class. How you set up your room will also suggest the style of learning and the environment you wish to convey.

Space

Space represents something more than a place to put things. To you, it represents a place to live, develop, grow, enjoy, learn, become. It becomes your responsibility to keep it fluid, alive, functional and meaningful.

Even if your room is cluttered upon your arrival, see it first as an empty area. You, the facilitator, are going to put things, ideas, curriculum, and attitudes into this room. This classroom will be the stage upon which your students perform. When the curtain goes up on that first day, your stage should be set with equipment and materials that you see as necessary to tuning the individual children into your program. As a first step, get to know your custodian. You will be needing to store some of the white elephants left you by a well-meaning teacher.

Use your chalkboard and draw yourself an empty area. Now fill in the space. Draw in closets, doors, obstructions that cannot be moved or removed. Draw in the porch or outside areas that might become an extension of your classroom. Draw in the electric outlets, the sink if you have one. Think of your water and electric areas in terms of their possible uses. What needs would best utilize the sink area? Your grade assignment, your curriculum, your children, your values will help you put this utility into use. Think about water—water to wash with, to mix with, to drink, to play and experiment with, to cook with. It's your water, your room, your curriculum, your individual program. How will you utilize it? Make this judgment for all of the

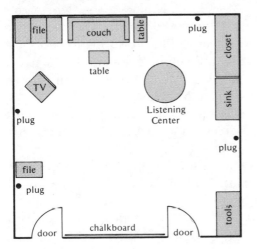

electric outlets as well. Organize your electrical equipment around these outlets.

Look at your space again, and try to think how best to conserve it. Remember, when thirty or thirty-five bodies start shuffling around in there it fills up fast. Some other things you may wish to consider are:

1   Where will you seat 30 to 35 children? Or will you?

2   Will each child have his own desk or will you use work areas and a rotation system with periods of time being spent at different stations?

3   Do you wish to save enough floor space for a large, flexible, open area that is multipurpose?

4   Can children be permitted after the first few weeks to move desks near friends or set up their own seating arrangements? I call this technique Scramble and set the following rules:

a   Certain things will not be moved. I name them: TV because of plug, tool chest near patio, etc.

b   You can move near anyone so long as you all agree.

c   I will always get your immediate eye-to-eye, mouth-closed attention when I dim the lights or say "Stop."

Materials and Activities

In an individualized program it is important to have things to do, things that a child can go to independently, keys for self-correction. Students will be expected to learn from and with each other. As the facilitator, you should never appear to be working harder than the children, answering questions that children could answer, thinking for the child. The job of the facilitator is to have the all-knowing eye, keep the ball rolling, become attuned to the child who is soon to become a problem due to lack of self-motivation, get materials into the hands of children before or as they need them, talk over problems in private, maintain a productive, suitable climate in which to work.

Your interest centers will depend on you, your grade level, the materials you have available, the freedom given you by your principal, your commitment to others on the staff (do you have to team, departmentalize, co-teach?). Suggestions for materials come from magazines like Grade Teacher, Instructor, and related professional journals, by visiting classrooms at your school and at others, by telling, talking and asking your associates, and just by getting an idea, giving it wings, and letting it fly. Ideas are all around us, on television, in movies, from children's interests, from a parent's suggestion. Remember that very few ideas are truly original; probably the teacher whose idea you feel you are taking took it from someone else who took it from someone else and embellished it. When you walk through someone else's room you may see a thousand ideas, but until what you see has meaning to you in relation to the needs of your children you will pass it by.

This is another way of saying that you can't completely set up your interest centers in advance. My belief is that interest centers are born, not created by the teacher. When the needs and interests of your children become more apparent, you can feed into those interests more directly. For example, if some children are interested in gadgets bring in some old broken clocks, radios, generators, record players, toasters. Provide pliers, screwdrivers, tape, encourage an idea for an invention (if they do not already have one), and let them fool around. Many a highway engineer was born while adventuring in a sandbox in kindergarten. Slot car collectors can be encouraged to design or re-design their own cars, make models from clay or balsa wood, create drawings and diagrams. Once set on fire with an idea to pursue, the children will bring all educational skills into play.

Get stuff, plenty of stuff, leave it around in willing hands, and it will grow into giant projects. Just don't get more things in your room than you can reasonably govern, and always be safety conscious. Expect responsible conduct and a willingness and pride from the children in maintaining their own room.

When you think your room is ready, walk around, sit in the children's chairs. Get a perspective from their world. Scale the room down if necessary. And prepare to be fluid. Don't change just to be changing, but if a change becomes necessary as time goes by, make it. If something proves to be no good, toss it out. Don't stay with something that died a long time ago. If you find the children do not take to something you thought was great, put it away. Maybe the timing is wrong. You can't sell if nobody is buying.

YOUR VERY FIRST DAY

The excitement of the first day is a form of stage fright that no teacher ever really overcomes. This is one of the joys of the profession. Yes, you have a pack of attendance cards and a pack of children, usually numbering somewhere between thirty and forty by count. Sometimes you know the children, more often you don't. Even in a school where you know faces and names and the students know you, you are really strangers. You must not *assume* that you really know these kids. Go slowly, tread gently. Be aware.

Getting Acquainted

You might begin by casually visiting with the children and encouraging them to visit with their classmates. Let them choose the seat they wish. Have them make name cards and wear them. Help them get to know each other. At this time, I discuss the philosophy behind my Scramble technique and excite them about the near future (usually the following week), when they may elect to sit by those with whom they work best and whom they most enjoy.

Getting Straight

It is important that you not let the class get away from you. If it is going to take direction, be sure you have some say in the way it will go. Any teacher who has ever lost a class from under her does approach cautiously. I do not mean to suggest that one becomes a ruler-slapping tyrant, but you are the director and it is easier to call the shots in the beginning than pull a class back later. I might even go so far as to quote from the teacher's grapevine of wisdom: Be fair, firm, and friendly.

It helps if you can pretty well establish what is acceptable and unacceptable. This can be done in a manner comfortable and natural to you. My method is to be honest, explaining to the children that this room is their home, their place of business, their castle, their ship, but there is just *one captain,* even though there may be many leaders. We discuss this. I may relate it to the rules in team sports or to the number of chief cooks in a kitchen, but I get this message across. I usually like to tell them that I am their captain just as the Principal is mine and Superintendent is his. I point out that ours is a classroom of the students, by the students, and for the students, but I am still overseer because total responsibility for their safety and instruction cannot be delegated. It is not the child but the credentialed teacher who must answer to the system.

Along with my chatting I try to convey to them that teachers are human beings and that they need to be aware that, like parents, we have good and bad days and it will benefit them to be perceptive as to how *all* their neighbors, including teachers, feel. We talk about "bugging others" and the golden rule: Treat others as you would like to be treated. I tell them that if they are not conducting themselves in a *businesslike way,* they can expect to be asked to stand outside. (This draws a smirk or two until I remind them that a businesslike operation will "dock" the child for time misused. We are in this game for profit.) I seldom have to enforce this rule, as I do not send a child out without some earlier personal/private warning. In a well-organized structure a teacher need only give a hand gesture for lowering the voice or merely walk to the child. I do not wish to give the impression that my room is silent at all times. What I am saying is that noise and quiet are relative terms used in the context of what is being done. I simply make a rule of thumb that "when you are doing something that interferes with the activity and application of another, you are not being considerate, and to me that is not businesslike behavior."

Getting Organized

You will find that you will need to develop some methods for organizing time and for organizing the children's work. I explain to the children that the schedule for the day will always be written on the board. I also explain that the schedule will vary from day to day and that they should learn to check the board each morning. The Appendix to this chapter provides a sample schedule for the first day.

On this first day, I give every child in the room a three-ring binder and a supply of paper, both plain and lined, and explain that the binder is to be organized into sections with tabs. The binders will contain math worksheets, a list of books read, short stories written, spelling quizzes, and sections of special interest, such as cartoons, poetry, letters to friends, and so forth. I have found that often there is so much activity in some binders that the material must be removed and bound separately. Parents find the volumes exciting.

Diagnosing the Children

It is important that you begin to assess the needs, capabilities, and limitations of your students as soon as possible. On the first day, I begin to interview each child, asking him to tell me about his home, hobbies, vacations, friends, clubs, travel, sports, animals, and so forth. I try to evaluate his needs and his level of confidence as he speaks.

Some other ways in which I begin to diagnose the children are as follows: I listen to them speak and read, ask them to write and compute, watch them socialize, and look for evidence of empathy with others, of original thinking, of common sense, of sense of worth, and of ability to take responsibility.

KEEPING IT TOGETHER

Once the hurdle of the first day is over and your program begins to expand from a tight routine toward individualization, a major concern will be keeping track of this new world you have created. Here are some suggestions which may help.

Equipment

Determine which equipment is noisy and which makes no noise and can be used without disturbing others. Experimenting with the use of noise and silence is the only way to provide harmony in the work environment. Hammers and saws are not conducive to quiet tasks such as reading, writing, and arithmetic. Sewing or clay modeling during quiet study yes, but hammering and sawing no.

After much of this trial and error you will develop a sophistication in interlacing activities, so that all the children can be comfortable.

You should develop an awareness of acceptable noise levels and move quickly to signal the class that they are approaching the excess limits. I turn off the lights when the limits have been reached. In time, children become aware of this acceptable noise level and will take on the responsibility of lowering the lights to alert the class themselves.

Equipment is expensive and no one should touch or try to operate it without being checked out by the teacher. My preference is to "hire" an equipment monitor rather than hold an election for this job. Once he has been designated to operate and check out a certain piece of equipment, the monitor's name is placed in sight on a roster where the class can contact him and either check out or report misuse of equipment.

It is to the benefit of each child in the classroom to work toward a variety of learning experiences and use of different media in the total development of his image. All children should be encouraged to use all equipment after proper checkout procedures.

Time

Some children are fully capable of organizing their time. Some need to develop this skill. When you are asked what a child is doing with his time you should have some accountable way of substantiating this, by producing either the actual work or a statement of what he has done. Contracts and checklists are helpful ways of indicating how time was spent. Here are two examples:

Contract
I, _____, agree to read 10 pages of _____ each day. Check if done.

	Yes	No
M		
T		
W		
Th		
F		

Checklist (indicate minutes)	M	T	W	Th	F
Reading					
Story Writing					
Math Kit					
Drawing					
Listening Corner					
Chess					
Construction					
Phys. Ed.					
Spelling					
Name			Week Ending		

Keeping Records

The children's binders, mentioned above, provide very helpful indications of their academic progress. In addition, I use several other records as well:

Anecdotal Records These are most helpful. I write quotes, attendance, attitudes, successes, insecurities, observations, test scores—anything that pertains to the understanding of the total child. To this, I add home contacts, guidance, health information. I indicate the successes that children report during conferences with them.

Attendance Cards   Two categories of attendance are reported. Illness (excused) or non-illness (non-excused and not supported by state money). I follow through on non-excused absences immediately and record all reasons for absence on the back of the card. This creates a handy reference for office and medical referral.

Contracts   I make a learning contract with each child, which will be acceptable to us both. I use these as a counseling tool in talking with individual students about setting goals for themselves and using their time profitably.

Cumulative and Health Records   I scan these for any pertinent information that may concern the child, for comments on his behavior by past teachers to see if a pattern of behavior becomes evident.

Parent Conferences   I do keep in touch with the home. I encourage any parent to visit without appointment and take an interest in the education of his child. I use the parent–teacher conference as our first report session and use a checklist-type report card as our second, third, and final report. I do not give letter grades. In assessing the child, I try to see the whole child in relation to his health, his environment, his learning needs, his social development.

MY FAVORITE YEAR

This last year of teaching stood out among ten for me. Perhaps in sharing it with you, I can pass along some of the excitement that comes with teaching. This year will never be repeated no matter how hard I try to copy what I did. The children will be gone, the spirit they supplied replaced by new children. There will be other classes, and they will be good ones, but I wonder if I am the only teacher in the world with a memory of my pet class tucked secretly down deep in my heart.

The class was self-motivated, working at a level unthreatening to them, encouraged by their peers, and they grew in the skills of reading, handwriting, mathematics, story writing, and meaningful conversation. In addition, they experimented with television, hammer and nails, recording devices, dramatic play, drafting techniques, chess, checkers, jacks, knitting, cooking, library walks, field trips, a class newspaper, singing, dancing, dreaming, planning, poetry writing, letter writing, drawing, painting, modeling with clay, student government, resource room visits, and playground activities.

They were fourth, fifth, and sixth graders. Half were girls, half boys. Later analysis indicated that the reading span went from early primary through grade nine. I wanted to individualize and I wanted to take each child from where he was. I liked to call it a nongraded classroom and threw the words around in an all-knowing manner, but I never really was able to cast off fully grade-level labels, what with class placement cards, recess schedules, lunch periods, etc. I did have my fun when visitors came because they could never tell who was in which grade by size, academic ability, and maturity. Even the kids found that special fun. I had brought along a chosen ten students from my previous fourth grade to become the fifth graders. The fourth and sixth graders were assigned because past teachers felt that they would benefit by my teaching style and the plan for individualization. Some children asked to be assigned. Many of the children had feelings of defeat, poor peer relationships, and very poor self-images.

Our reading program was based on books chosen by the students from the public library each twenty-one days, each child taking out and trying to read a total of six books during that period. Everyone read. Our book reports were mostly oral with the purpose of dramatizing or selling the book. I listed each book reported upon and the number of pages in each. If we did not know a word we went to anyone and everyone who could help us. We took responsibility to help each other and voluntarily joined into cohesive work units. Those who were reading very well had steady jobs and enjoyed the status that it brought. We tried words on. We kept saying the word over and over (in context) until it made sense. We learned to proofread. Our policy was to ask our friends and classmates before coming to the teacher for help. It is amazing how many answers can be obtained or problems resolved without involving the teacher. I often avoided answering by saying, "Ask somebody else."

I worked very hard at phasing myself out of certain responsibilities that I felt they could handle. Abdicating the trivia, I used my time to listen, encourage, and counsel. The one area in which I was most helpful was putting what they needed into their hands so that a project could be completed.

In the file cabinet, available to all, were worksheets and suggestions for projects. Within the year many types of contracts and record-keeping devices were attempted. But as we became more sophisticated in using these, we discovered that one cannot departmentalize learning into categories. For example, if you are reading a book about Dr. Jonas Salk, do you mark this activity down as reading, science, discovery, or health? Even in doing something as definite as the Math Kit, children would ask, "Am I doing math or handwriting?" The answer is, "Both." Each skill is part of the whole of knowledge. Some things we were able to be definite about: so many words in a story (we could count these), so many lessons in the Math Kit (we could count these), so many pages in a book read (we could count these); and strangely enough we ended up with reading, writing, and arithmetic.

And I haven't said anything about the quality of what we did! One haiku poem could be far greater in quality than one thousand words written uncaringly. Or maybe that child sitting quietly in a corner was dreaming up some way to feed the hungry of the world, dispose of smog, or design a safe automobile or highway. Whatever happened to that teacher who threw Thomas Edison out of school for daydreaming?

No special grouping was demanded within the classroom other than that evident from the child's own selection or decision to perform at a given level. Any pressure to perform came from the child himself or from the peer group with which he chose to align himself. All were self-motivated; some appeared to be *self-driven*. Strangely enough, it was obvious that the child knew better what he sought than I did. It left me with the knowledge that personality styles develop very early.

Motivation to begin work came after morning business when I asked each student individually what tasks he planned to attempt during the day. When it was evident that each had some pattern for the day I said, "Go to work." Having a general idea of what each expected to accomplish, I used my time to help the laggers and keep poor planners on the track.

Group goals were one hour for reading, another for math, and an extra hour for reading alone. We used the buddy system for correcting writing or for proofreading. All the students took on a willingness to help those who knew less than they and shared their expertise in tutoring those who needed help. There was pride in giving as well as receiving help. The students remained interested and motivated.

I accepted and listened to all ideas and encouraged those that seemed safe for the student. Students took on responsibility for planning drama, dances, swim parties, and treats at school. They took care of room environment and decoration. In time, we scrambled so that the wall territory over a desk area belonged to that student, who had the privilege of decorating and maintaining that area from floor to ceiling if he chose. We set up dress design displays, spacecraft displays, hot car bulletin boards. It was original and represented student interests.

The second semester brought us a talented student teacher who was strong in music, energetic in attempting new ideas. The children fell in love with her, and I stepped back often to let her grow and give of herself to the class. She often took groups of five for a nature walk, cooking adventure, or music lessons. I felt good that I had the privilege to allow a student teacher to feel right about entering the profession.

Parents were welcome anytime. One parent came weekly to work with a group interested in her art field. One parent, a doctor in cancer research, developed mini-courses at the level of those interested. These covered drug abuse, animal observation, and so forth.

My experiences in the classroom described have provided me with the opportunity of knowing children deeply and meaningfully. The need to listen to children is still of the highest priority. More and more children are expressing the need to be themselves and develop in a manner valuable to their future. They do not want us to do the job for them and create them in our image. They want to do it themselves and will seek our guidance if we make ourselves available.

APPENDIX: SAMPLE FIRST-DAY SCHEDULE

8:25– 8:30	Enter. Ready for flag salute.
8:30– 8:50	Attendance. Class business. Getting acquainted.
8:50– 9:30	A solid subject, such as math. (Use work for diagnosis of readiness levels.)
9:30– 9:50	Recess. (Before class leaves for recess indicate how you wish class to return to room and what assignment will be.)
9:50–10:15	A writing assignment (short story, poetry). "Don't worry about spelling. This is the *rough copy*. Try to write so it can be read. Count number of words at end of assignment and circle the count. Pencils are on your desk, extra paper here. If you finish ahead of time, illustrate your story or poem. Do not disturb your neighbor. Raise your hand when finished, and I will pick up your paper." (Use this time to watch children and their work habits and attention span.)

10:15–10:30	A walk with teacher around the campus—office, nurse's room, lost and found, athletic equipment area, bathrooms, cafeteria, bus stop, crossings, assigned playground areas, special classrooms such as resource, opportunity, ESL (English as a Second Language).
10:30–11:00	More writing. Have students complete permission slips. Homework is to take them home to be signed. "This is your first lesson in responsibility." Discuss ways to be successful in this assignment. "It must get home, it must get signed, it must come back tomorrow. Who can remember?"
11:00–11:30	Distribute binders with binder paper. Discuss organization of binder. Standards are that it does not go home, it will be looked at frequently by the teacher, papers will be dated and all work chronologically filed by subject matter. Explain in detail. Be serious. Show examples. Explain that this binder is a partial portrait of the artist.
11:30–12:30	LUNCH HOUR. (Again, explain standards.)
12:30– 1:15	First two or three minutes are spent at desk, head down, or relaxing. No talking, no visiting. Reason twofold: Children are hot or tired or keyed up, and time to change gears from fast to quiet activity. Body needs a few minutes to do job. When the children are ready to work, read short stories written in the morning. Introduction to purpose of reading story. "Read with feeling, hold interest of class, be articulate, project voice, hope you can read your own writing." Stories may be collected and dittoed, used next day to try proofreading of a neighbor's paper. Many uses for these papers. Eventually they will be filed in the child's binder.
1:15– 1:30	TV for instruction. Some fun follow-up.
1:30– 2:00	Drawing a design about the mood or the theme of the program. Put all the work up on bulletin boards that day after school to show students, not teachers.
2:00– 2:30	P.E. Let girls play girls, boys play boys. Select captains by count-offs, odd numbers, even numbers.
2:30– 3:10	Evaluation of the day. Plan for tomorrow. Remind about homework. Clean up room. Walk class to bus if busing.

CHAPTER 2
PERSONALIZED LEARNING

Darlene Atteberry

This chapter spells out quite explicitly one teacher's approach to what she calls "personalized learning." A rationale plus a methodology of teaching and learning accompany the discussion of a wide range of activities, techniques, materials, and use of community resources. This teacher moves from a structured classroom into an initiation period, in which both she and the children learn about student needs, interests, and abilities. The chapter shares some valuable insights, questions, and problems involved in practicing personalized learning for the upper grades.

As an "innovative" teacher, I have found that one of the greatest obstacles to my innovations has been the difference between my philosophy of education and the philosophy of the majority—the community, the administration, the board of education, and other teachers. My view—that education must become more relevant—often seems to be in opposition to the view of this majority, who want education to be the same as it was when they were in school, whether that was five or fifty years ago. Consequently, when such people view my classroom they equate the activities with "playing and talking" rather than learning. They are struck so immediately by the difference between my classroom and the traditional classroom to which they are accustomed that they cannot see what is, in fact, happening.

I must readily admit that too often fads have developed in education, soon to be forgotten because they were never organized well enough to become effective. Consequently, those of us who want change are always in danger of succumbing to the majority. Unless we are to become "historical artifacts" (while we're still alive!), we must become organized among ourselves, at least to the point of being able to communicate our purposes to others in order that they can understand our goals for students.

It is for this reason that before discussing my program for personalized learning I have set down some brief statements about my methods and about the curricular objectives toward which I strive. I have found, for example, that the doubting classroom visitor becomes much more receptive to the sight of several children cooking in one corner when he understands my mathematics objectives. The same holds true for construction as it relates to mathematics and following directions.

MY METHOD

I cannot tolerate the idea of children having to endure a system of education in which boredom and irrelevance abound. If I do nothing else in my teaching career, I will try to change these two factors.

I try to conquer boredom by presenting a wide range of activities in every area of my curriculum. I also do many things that are not associated with schooling at present. My classes take trips to nearby businesses and public services. We invite people of different professions into our room. We have many picnics and just plain "time to talk" in the park. We cook and sew in the room. So much learning can emerge from these activities without the children being aware that they are learning. You may say, "Why shouldn't the child be made aware that he's learning?" I would say, "Because 'learning' probably has meant unpleasant experiences for him for many years." Besides, eventually it will dawn on the student that he has learned something.

I try to make education more relevant to these young people by involving them in what is learned. I believe if you discuss with children what they know as opposed to what they do not know, they will realize what things they *want* to know. I try to get them to understand that they must start from where they are (from what they know) and build their learning from there.

Once the children are involved in class discussions and decision-making sessions we can arrive at a mutually acceptable curriculum. Believe it or not, my Objectives List and the ideas of the children are very similar. I think this is because their desires and mine are related to everyday living. Sometimes there are some things I think they should know that they may not mention. In such a case, as a member of the discussion group I might present the question "Do you know . . . ?" and work into that area to find out how much they already know and how much they each need to know.

OUR OBJECTIVES

To give you a sample of the kind of Objectives List from which I work, I have included a few objectives from various areas of the curriculum. It should be noted that these examples are drawn from a fourth grade class.

Math Objectives

Most important, to give children the realization that math is a part of everyday living, not just book and paper drills.

To teach concepts of measurement—liquid measurement, dry measurement, and linear measurement, including the metric system.

To teach basic geometry—recognition of shapes, knowledge of how to find perimeters, the concept of how geometry is used in our physical world.

To teach the concept of fractions—fractions used in cooking and in linear measurement.

To review, re-teach, and strive for a high level of competency in addition and subtraction.

To introduce and re-teach multiplication and division, striving for understanding, not just rote learning.

Language Objectives

Most important, to give children a chance to put their own thoughts into words, through stories, letters, poems.

To teach proper use of capitalization.

To teach use of some punctuation—periods, question marks, quotation marks, commas, etc.

To teach the concept that a sentence is one complete statement (to help children overcome their tendency to write run-on sentences).

To introduce the concept of paragraphing.

To teach proper form for letter writing and addressing of envelopes.

Reading Objectives

Most important, to develop enjoyment of reading.

To teach that reading is used in many different ways—reading for information, reading for facts, reading for relaxation and escape.

To continue emphasizing various decoding skills.

To help develop comprehension.

To help each child realize his own reading ability and select books carefully.

Social Studies Objectives

To teach the concept of self and the importance of self-responsibility. All other social studies objectives evolve from this important basis, including:

The role of each child in the classroom—responsibility for discipline; sharing of custodial duties; importance of making wants and needs felt.

The role of the child in the community and the role of other community members; how the community relates to the state; the concept of a state as opposed to a country; a country as it relates to other countries politically, economically, and geographically; discussion about current events.

GETTING UNDER WAY

With the foregoing remarks concerning my purposes and methods as a foundation, I would like to explain how I organize and maintain my program for personalized learning.

The Summer Before

It usually takes about a week to set up my room before the students arrive. However, I use about a month for general preparation. Initially, I identify the learning centers I want to make available to the students in order to orient them to the new year, the new teacher, and perhaps the new philosophy under which I operate. I like to offer a wide variety of centers so that each child may have a chance to find an area of success and/or interest. Here are some examples of center combinations I have used: measuring center, art area, creative writing area, reading center, science corner, and map-making area, or, a little less conventionally, cooking corner, construction cranny, book nook, summer sharing center, classroom publisher's place, and sound studio (musical instruments, tape recorder, and record player). One year, I merely set up the furniture into areas and let the children decide what areas they wanted to designate. After they decided, we all put the materials where we thought they belonged. My reaction to this last technique is that its success depends on the background of the students. If they are accustomed to a traditional approach, they will probably react as mine did and produce very traditional centers. However, if the students have been able to make some learning choices in the past, they will probably have more original ideas.

Whether I make the decisions about the first centers appearing in the room or not, I collect appropriate materials to place into the centers. The schools where I have worked have not been overly stocked with anything except textbooks, the items I use the least! Therefore, I have learned to devise, beg, borrow, and liberate learning materials from a variety of sources. This may not be conducive to the most beautiful-looking classroom, if commercial neatness describes classroom beauty, but it is conducive to creativity within an active environment, and this is vital to my philosophy.

I collect these materials during the summer from friends and by visiting stores' throw-away bins. I buy some of the inexpensive things, and then, after the school year begins, I rely upon the parents and relatives of my students for additional materials. In addition, I save materials which are usable from year to year. A list of materials I like to have is included in the Appendix to this chapter.

The materials I borrow are things like library books from the public library, films and filmstrips from the audio-visual lab in the district, games and teaching materials from other teachers. Some items like countertop broiler ovens and sewing machines are borrowed from friends who say, "Use them as much as necessary but, if you go away, please return them so I can make sure someone else will have a chance to use them." Although much of this borrowing must take place during the school year, summer is the time to prepare lists of available materials and methods of recording who borrows things and from whom. These records are necessary because many times the children will borrow things for use by class members and they must be noted in order to be returned when necessary.

Summer is also a good time to make contacts for the school year. I spread the word about my program to as many people as possible. Businessmen are a source of many opportunities for learning. They will often save items which I deem useful in a classroom, or they can suggest where to get an item. They have information about the business world which comes in handy in math, social studies, and other related topics. They may also agree to be guest speakers or conduct a tour of their businesses.

City officials are also great resources as speakers, disseminators of literature about the local government, and tour guides of the local environment in which the government of the city operates. Radio stations, television stations, newspapers, and other available media centers often provide interesting speakers as well as tours.

If these people know the kinds of educational practice you value, they are more than willing to offer their services. However, it is very important to be honest and thorough when explaining your program or they may not be willing to help. Some general courtesies help, too. Letters of invitation from the children, pictures, or thank-you letters let the person know how much his time and effort are appreciated.

I also utilize the summer hours to make games and other teaching aids for the year. There are some good ideas to be obtained from visits to other rooms and other schools during the year and from books and summer workshops which are gradually becoming more available on the subject of individualized instruction. I might add that some of these workshops are good motivators at the end of the summer to get rolling into the school year.

The last part of the summer, before the children arrive, I spend arranging the physical environment of the room. I generally begin with a diagram of the room and locations of materials and furniture. These diagrams serve several purposes. They serve as a check to make sure I have allowed for all of the areas needed, they give me direction when I actually start moving things, and they serve as references later when I want to see how the room has been arranged at various times during the school year or when I need a new idea for a change of environment. During the year these diagrams serve another purpose. They show students where to put the furniture either as a result of my decision to rearrange things or as a result of their input which I have diagrammed for them. Many times, the students have also diagrammed changes. Figure 2.1 shows a diagram of the room as it appears at the beginning of the year. Figure 2.2 is an example of how the room may look after the program is under way.

When arranging the room, I have some basic ideas in mind. The room must be efficient. I do not want any unnecessary furniture in the room. All materials must have a place and be marked so that the children can find them. The room must be arranged to accommodate a wide variety of activities; therefore, it must be flexible. And, most im-

FIGURE 2.1   ROOM DIAGRAM

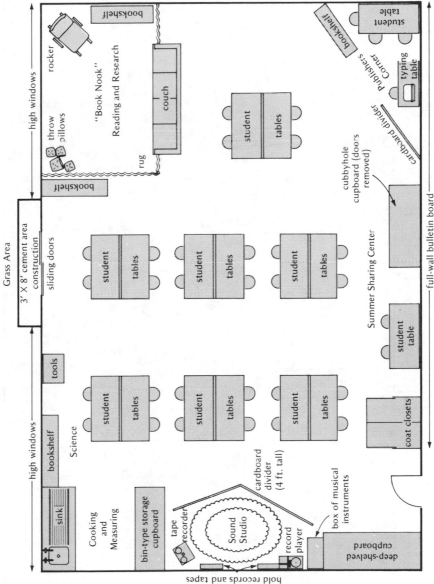

FIGURE 2.2   ROOM DIAGRAM

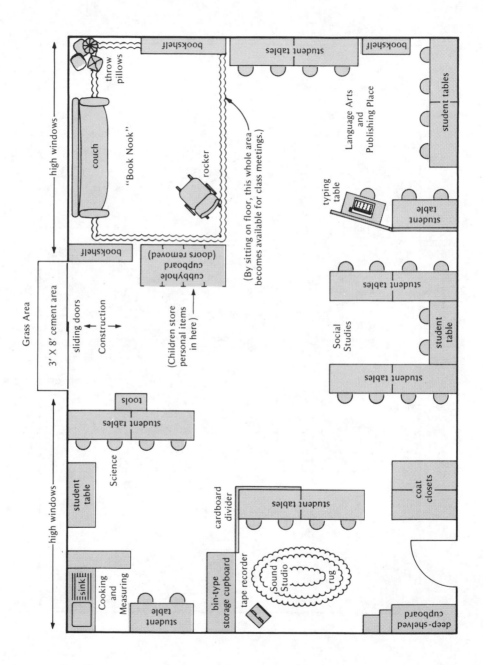

portant, the room must be arranged to facilitate the needs of the children and the methods of the teacher.

Working into Personalized Learning

The method I have developed the last two years has worked well for me. In the beginning of the year I remain rather structured. We do several all-class activities each day for the first two weeks or so. I like to keep a tighter structure initially so that I can develop some discipline patterns with the children. When I don't do this, I find the children will not listen to me at all, and discipline becomes a problem. This two-week period also allows me a chance to become acquainted with the children and helps the children to know each other. (I like to develop a "we-ness" so that the students will know I will support and help them. I hope they will support and help each other also.) When children have come from classrooms where everything has been planned for them and the teacher does most of the talking, they are afraid to help each other. They seem to feel it's wrong and equate it with "cheating." I have to create an atmosphere that indicates that helping each other to learn is good.

Some of the activities that help make a change come about are these: As a sort of mini–Social Studies unit, we choose partners and "research" each other. We learn a lot about each other's likes, dislikes, families, interests, etc. Charts can be made of *Interests in Our Room, Names of Our Families, Hobbies We Share,* and other topics of interest. It's also fun to put up riddles about each other on the bulletin boards and try to solve them; for example, "This person has blue eyes and blond hair. He likes baseball and football best. His family has five people. Who is he? _____." (I have names cut out, and children pin the name with the riddle where they think it belongs. Then, after a few days I can see how many are answered correctly.) The children can look at the charts for information to solve the riddles or ask the child who they think fits the riddle's description. The only thing the questioned child can't say is, "Yes, I'm the one!"

This initiation period is a good time to introduce the games and manipulative materials available in the room. I usually introduce a couple of familiar games, then a couple of new ones. Immediately following I let the children choose which game they would like to play, and we all play for a while. When the game session is over, since everyone was playing it gives me a good opportunity to stress clean-up and checking games for all of the parts. If picking up is not stressed very strongly right from the start, the games will not last long, and some good activities will be ended. Games are a good way to get feelings of cooperation started and a chance for strangers to talk while playing.

With regard to academic subjects: During the first two weeks I like to give the kids a chance to "get into the swing" again. More likely than not, for three months they have not done any math, writing, or reading. Too often, I see teachers using the first weeks to test and place the children in "appropriate" books. I think it's more advantageous to use this time to reacquaint them with the classroom. Since many children will be all too familiar with "book learning," this is a good time to introduce other ways of learning. In our district there are many films and records available in math, reading, science, etc. I order a few for the beginning of the year, and we view them and talk about the possible learnings. Then I show the students how to order from the catalog, and from then on they order for themselves. I also show many kinds of reading materials—books, word cards, games, and so forth. In math I show them where the manipulative materials are located, and we talk about the possibilities for their use. I do similar things in other areas. All of the time, however, I try to keep their ideas and suggestions foremost and keep them thinking of other possibilities for learning experiences.

The purposes of the initiation period are to familiarize the students with a wide variety of means and modes of learning and to familiarize myself with the new students' needs, interests, and abilities. The size of the class, the degree of independence shared by the students, and the amounts of new materials to present determine the length of this period. Other kinds of activities appropriate for the initiation are:

—Trips around the school to acquaint the students with available facilities, boundaries, and personnel.

—Exploratory periods in the learning center, the library, or other available rooms, to help familiarize the students with other learning resources.

—Structured assignments to test for particular learnings with follow-up sessions in which the discussion centers upon ways the same learning could be shown independently, in small groups, and with other media.

—Opportunities to participate in small groups with many purposes from problem-solving to discussion. These give many students chances to work together and a chance to see where various group strengths lie.

If workbooks are required in some subjects, this initiation period is also a good time to make sure the students can use them properly and independently, building in learning extensions so that the books do not become a competitive activity, with the quality of learning becoming secondary.

Gradually I try to wean the children away from this structure. I have been most successful doing it gradually because when I've tried to do it too fast, I've ended up with complaints from parents, broken equipment, bored and disoriented children, and a generally unpleasant atmosphere. Therefore, I usually start by taking a certain time period each day and let the children choose what they are going to do during this time. (The younger the children, the shorter the period.) I usually let everyone make his choice independently. If I see that some children are not progressing well, then I help them choose or make the choices for them. Sometimes it helps to give such children two choices from which to make their selection.

I think every student should have the opportunity to make his own choices; however, if a child cannot choose effectively, the teacher is still responsible for learning. If the child is not showing signs of learning, then it is the teacher's responsibility to guide him until he can learn to make his own choices. For some children, this may take months. However, the teacher must not assume he will never choose appropriate ways of learning and thus remove all choices. Instead, the teacher and student must identify where and how appropriate choices are made and allow freedom there. Then, both teacher and student can gradually build a greater selection as competence is demonstrated by the student. I am not talking only about students who have been slow learners or who have performed poorly. Any student can have problems with self-selection, depending on how much experience he has had with making his own decisions.

Orienting the Parents

One of the methods I use for communicating with parents is a dittoed letter. I write these letters about every two months. In them, I include information about the activities going on in the classroom, any special studies going on, and requests for anything we might need from time to time. I try to keep the letters informal and often put in little jokes and personal trivia.

Many parents who work and don't get to school often say that this really makes them feel that they know what's going on. Two of the most important letters are the one I send the first day of the year, explaining what I have planned for the year, and the last one, which summarizes what actually took place.

Diagnosing the Children

I think one of the most important aspects of diagnosis is to be sure all symptoms are taken into account. As a result, I use many methods of diagnosis. My own observation, feedback from students and parents (written and verbal, formal and informal), previous health records, and results of standardized and teacher-made tests—all these provide me with adequate assessment techniques.

Through these methods, I can assess the student's background, skills and comprehensions, how he learns best, and in what direction he is headed. Specifically, I want some knowledge about his skills and comprehension within subject matter areas—but not without the other factors. All aspects of the child's "learning style" must be considered.

The information gained will also be useful for conferences, for assessing directions to aim a child if necessary, and for providing parents, the student, and me an opportunity to see where our goals are similar and where they differ.

Observation techniques I use range from listening to individual students read to others, to direct question–answer sessions with me. I do not consider the latter to be test situations because of the atmosphere which I try to set. The students are made to realize that these are mutually beneficial; I can tell where the student's attempts have been successful and where they have not, as well as being able to assess where more teacher input would be helpful and where it would be a hindrance. Since I use a lot of parent volunteers in my program, there is time for individual conferences, and those I cannot do can be picked up by the volunteers when they are taught what cues I am looking for during conferences. Many methods can be used for scheduling conferences. I find a sign-up sheet to be the most useful. In a separate book which is always available to the students, I record the conferences. If a student neglects the responsibility of signing up for a conference, I sometimes make a red star showing him it is due. At other times, I just sign the student's name on the chart instead of giving him the opportunity to do so.

I use the individual conferences for assessing skills in math and reading and checking transferability in math and comprehension in reading, but I also use them as opportunities to develop a rapport with the students. I listen to their problems and special experiences. In this way, I think the students have an opportunity to see that I have a sincere desire to help them and that I can understand many factors which influence their school behavior. But I also let them know I am going to do everything I can to keep their learning progressing. I will not allow other factors to overpower their learning if we can cooperatively prevent it.

ORGANIZING FOR LEARNING

Once I have had an opportunity to get to know the children and the children have become acquainted with me and the riches of the classroom, it is time to develop techniques which will be used throughout the year. Let me mention here that I think the success of an individualized program lies in a wide variety of techniques. Children tire of the same procedures and so does the teacher. Therefore, methods of acquiring knowledge or skills in an area may change monthly, quarterly, or even weekly.

Generally, each morning begins by taking care of the "office chores" necessary for running a classroom. The students run their own "self-government" program in order to take care of these tasks and any others they deem necessary. For example, they may want to have a sharing period, a "court case," or a special program. The "court case" refers to their methods of dealing with discipline problems which may arise. I try to allow the students the opportunity to handle all of the discipline problems by getting at the causes and assessing or not assessing punishment as necessary. This teaches the students that their behavior is important and affects more people than the teacher; therefore, they need to be held accountable to those people. The people who "hear" the cases can reflect upon their own feelings in a situation as well as make a judgment about what would help eliminate the poor conduct. By the second month of school, there are, as a rule, few cases and those are of an unusual nature. I think this improvement comes about because the students do not like peer pressure and they feel responsible for making the classroom a better place in which to operate.

After morning business is conducted (about a half hour—you must allow sufficient time or the process is ineffective), the day usually takes one of two directions. Sometimes we designate particular subjects for everyone to work on in the morning and in the afternoon. At other times we work on any subjects scheduled by individuals, with certain parts of the room designated for "quiet activities" and "noisy activities," or centers for particular interests.

Basically, each child proceeds according to his own plan. At first I may write in some requirements for everyone, then gradually eliminate them. But, generally, each student identifies what he is going to do and proceeds accordingly. Although I still use subject matter identification for heading assignment sheets or contracts, all subjects are woven together. If a student writes a book as a science project, it could conceivably involve language arts, reading, art, and spelling. As a result, several subjects would be covered in one project. The student may work on it all day or for several days, all periods or a few periods; but, instead of making this an isolated learning experience in science, he would be shown or probably would discover for himself the interrelationships of many skills going into the making of the book. At the same time, other students may be involved in specific learning experiences geared just for a math objective or a spelling skill.

Determination of the objectives for the students is a critical part of my program. Aside from the general objectives stated earlier, I also define objectives for each individual child. I try to involve the parents as well as the students in the formulation of the objectives, but sometimes it is hard to get parent input. To whatever extent possible, we do define each student's objectives. One student may like to set a course for the entire year while another may function better by setting smaller goals, say for a week or a month.

Examples of these goals:

Within four weeks, the student will be able to multiply two-digit numbers by two-digit numbers with 90 percent accuracy.

By the end of the year, the student will be able to construct a small computer and describe how it functions.

By the end of the quarter, the student will have written at least forty different selections and have collected them in a scrapbook.

Before next week, the student will be able to pass the one-digit addition test.

By the end of the year, the student will be able to select books which he can read with good comprehension and will select at least one book to read per week.

During the year, the student will show the ability to avoid physical confrontation when an adverse situation arises.

By the end of the week, the student will be able to write a paragraph containing one main idea.

By the end of the year, the student will be using cursive writing more often than printing.

These goals may cover many areas and many kinds of achievement. At some times just getting the student involved may be enough, while at others quality of involvement may be the goal. Some goals will be achieved more readily than anticipated. This becomes a learning experience, too. Instead of assigning "busy work" to fill out the extra time, a conference is scheduled and new goals set. Similarly, too little time may be allotted one goal, and then extensions must be determined. However, it is essential to work with the child in these decisions so that they have meaning to him instead of being externally imposed by the teacher.

Once the objectives are determined, the child may select the modes of attaining them, depending upon his ability to do so, as previously mentioned. I keep track of how the children are progressing by looking at their contracts and assignment sheets and through the conferences. Many times the conferences do not have to be individual because several students may be working on similar topics. In these cases it is much more expedient and useful to have the conference in a group.

Small groups are a very useful means of helping students with common needs. I use a wide variety of groups depending upon the needs expressed by my students. The groups constantly vary, and students are placed in groups for many reasons. For example, a student who is proficient at relatively simple addition may be placed in a group in order to give him a chance to interact successfully because he needs group approval or because he needs to build his own self-image. Another student may be placed in the group because he may have a better way of communicating with the students in the group than I would as an adult. A student may not always be in a group dealing with a subject in which he is having difficulty because he may function better alone or he may tend to be associated with "poorer" students too often and need to break the trend.

Amid the individual and small-group activities, I like to intersperse large-group activities as well. After all, man is a social being and has a need to participate in large groups. I provide these large-group experiences in a variety of ways. Daily, there are large-group experiences at the morning business meetings. Then after lunch I always take time to read to the students for about fifteen minutes, and at the end of the day we all sit down for about fifteen minutes and discuss the day's successes and failures and their implications for the next day. Aside from these group experiences, occasionally we all embark on a social studies unit together, take walking trips together, sing, do similar art activities, or go to the park and have a picnic. At other times, we may all write thank-you letters or write stories or poems together.

I think it is a healthy balance among individual activities, small groups, and large-group experiences which keeps interest alive in the class and encourages maximal learning.

Overall, if individualized or personalized instruction is to succeed in a classroom, I think active involvement by students, teacher, parents, and community is essential. Coupled with this involvement, a rich environment full of varied learning methods will keep the students interested in learning activities throughout the year.

APPENDIX: SUGGESTED LIST OF MATERIALS

Math

plastic fruits and vegetables
paper bags
toy or real cash register
receipt books
store signs (advertising)
baskets
measured containers from 1 pint to 1 gallon
pitchers (plastic)
cake and pie pans
funnels
weights
drawing compasses

bus, plane, train schedules
calendars
old refrigerator
old stove
clocks
scales
abacus
old dishes
stainless steel utensils
mixing bowls
pots and pans
measuring cups
measuring spoons
tape measure
yardsticks

aprons
toy money
dice
old maps

Construction

building blocks
popsicle sticks
cardboard
boxes with lids
woodworking tools
wheels (any size)
nails
screws
sawhorses
leftover paints

shellac
paint brushes

Science
eyedroppers
jars with lids
plastic containers/lids
flasks
test tubes
garden tools
small motors (could be
   broken)
wagons
small pocket mirrors
stethoscope
aquariums
fishbowls
turtle bowls
microscopes
microscope slides
specimen dishes
sponges
flowerpots
magnets
pulleys
hot plate
Bunsen burner
seed packages
wire
nuts and bolts
cotton
magnifying glasses
animal cages
beakers
dissecting instruments
batteries
any kind of nets
little light bulbs
   (Christmas, flash-
   light)
light switches

Sewing (costumes,
   puppets)
felt

thread
old dolls
scarves
knitting needles
crochet hooks
thimbles
buttons
old sewing machine
yarn
old iron
ironing board
zippers
old sheets
scrap cloth

Writing
pens
old typewriter
envelopes
stationery

Reading
comic books
decorator pillows
   (to relax while
   reading)
rugs
children's old
   magazines
children's old books
travel folders
pieces of carpeting
old stuffed chairs
old couch
children's encyclopedia
shelves
magazine racks
old telephone books
puppets
foreign language
   records and materials

Art
shirt boards
shoe boxes

string
rope
odd-shaped bottles and
   jars
turpentine
old candles
straws
pipe cleaners
cigar boxes
paint shirts
old stapler
hole puncher
colored chalk
shaker containers
   (like salt)
spray bottles
linoleum tiles
ceramic tiles
marbles

Miscellaneous
balls
anything from foreign
   countries
adding machine
egg timer
toy cars
toy boats
kitchen cooking
   utensils
children's games
old cameras
earphones
radios
phonograph records
buckets
dishpans
brooms
mops
toy trains and track
TV trays
step stool
small globes
checkers and boards
chessmen

CHAPTER 3

INDIVIDUALIZING READING
FOR PRIMARY CHILDREN

Myrna Perks

This teacher takes us through her yearly emergence from the traditional three-group approach to reading into a highly individualized program in a self-contained classroom. The chapter abounds
with specific suggestions for types of learning contracts and assigned and free-choice activities. The teacher attempting individualization for the first time may wonder how to keep track
of the whirlwind of activity. Numerous techniques and illustrations are provided, accompanied by rationales for using them.

The teacher who is individualizing for the first time is plagued with
doubts. "Am I teaching all the basic skills?"

The following plan for the individualization of reading is one that
I have used successfully as a member of a two-teacher team which
worked with sixty primary-level children. I have also used it when
working alone with thirty children at the primary level; and I have used
it in both graded and multi-age classrooms.

In the pages that follow, I have attempted to describe various
aspects of this plan, as well as to offer some suggestions for keeping
an individualized program under control on a day-to-day basis.

GROUPING

I begin each year with reading groups and gradually move to individualization. In my previous years of teaching, before attempting
individualization, I had always used the group method; and even now
I still feel most secure by beginning the year with groups. However,
my need to keep the groups together diminishes earlier in the school
year with every class.

Groups are originally formed on the basis of school reading records and my subjective assessment after several days of association with my new students. I make my assessment upon hearing the children read from standard texts, questioning them on comprehension of what was read, and gauging their phonetic word attack skills and ability to write simple sentences. I do not bother with any specific tests at this time because the groups can always be changed. My main purpose is to place the children, as nearly as possible, into homogeneous academic groups based on general reading skills. The children are then given a textbook and workbook. This arrangement gives me confidence that none of the children are being neglected and that each is acquiring the necessary skills as he works in his text.

The original groupings begin to change as the year progresses, to be replaced by other groups which are formed temporarily on the basis of need. Very short teacher-prepared skills tests, exchanged and corrected on the spot by the children, are used to diagnose needs. Children needing help in certain areas (using context clues, finding main ideas, recounting sequences of events, etc.) are grouped for a lesson. It soon becomes evident that often the children being grouped for a specific lesson are not in the same "sacred" reading group to which I had originally assigned them.

At the same time, the text I assigned begins to play a very minor role in the total program until by the end of the year it has no specific importance. The children proceed with their self-selected library books from class, school, or public libraries, and their assorted assigned worksheets for skill development.

The Buddy System

Another way in which the children are grouped is through what I call the "buddy system." Children enjoy reading to each other and doing worksheets together. I encourage this, and I am often amazed at how much learning takes place when they share in this manner. At the same time, some children may be somewhat reluctant to talk to other children in class. In this case, I arrange to have a child cooperate with one other student, and, as he gains confidence, I encourage him to adopt a buddy of his own choice. I make it clear that a buddy relationship can be maintained for as short or long a term as the child desires. However, the minimum term should allow each child to perform a mutual service for his buddy; for example, if Joe has read to Tom, Joe must listen to Tom read to him.

When it becomes obvious that the buddies are not conforming to the required task, I split them up. While I have no ironclad rule that each child have a buddy, it seems to help if I begin with buddies for everyone. If there is an odd number of children in the room, I make one cluster of three buddies.

MATERIALS AND ACTIVITIES

The children seem to be busier and work harder when they are given the freedom to select their own tasks rather than to follow a teacher's assignment—which in any case may just be busy work to do while the teacher is occupied with other students.

Providing this freedom of selection, however, does require quite a stock of materials. Some of the materials I use most are commercially prepared individualized reading programs; books from district libraries and a large assortment of supplementary texts for all levels; magazines, including adult magazines requested by the children, such as *Hot Rod* or *Quarterback;* stories recorded on tapes, to be listened to by children as they read along; a picture file, categorized by subject—animals, family, sports, etc.—to be used for story writing; and worksheets. One type of worksheet is placed under a sheet of acetate which can be written on with washable ink or crayon and wiped clean. A second type I make up myself and have the child copy the work onto another sheet so that the master will last longer.

Classroom Library—A Child-Oriented Task

Much of our activity in reading centers on our classroom library. At the beginning of the year I introduce all of my library books to the class and give them the choice of organizing and categorizing the library. Once the library is set up the children decide where any new books belong. Occasionally a book gets misplaced because John and Joe do not agree on the proper category, but this irons itself out in the course of the year.

An assortment of books and magazines is dumped on the floor in one heap, and the children are given the task of organizing our class library in two to three days. They decide on categories (not really my choice of classifications, but they are acceptable) and then decide which books belong on a particular shelf. When a classification is not clear-cut, the children have to decide and agree upon a classification. (For example, *The Three Bears* may be placed with animal stories or make-believe stories or easy books. Other shelves or sections include science books, riddles and jokes, magazines, fun books, hard books, true stories, and famous people.)

While the class is busy with seat work, each child is asked to come to the shelves and select a book he wants to read. This book is used in addition to the regular text assignment. As the year progresses it is possible for a child to omit the use of the text, basing his reading assignments on library books chosen for enjoyment only or as part of social studies or science research. My aim is to have the children read a book in one week, but some books take more or less time than that. Each week the class is called together and introduced to a teacher-made book report form. To bolster the student's interest, this procedure is repeated for several weeks with different forms, ranging from extremely easy forms (for example, forms to be colored) to more difficult written forms. There are over two dozen forms from which to choose. (See Appendix A for suggestions for alternative ways of making book reports and samples of book report forms.) Each child is free to use a previously used form or to try a new one. Initially, I explain the use of the new form. Then the children teach each other how to use the various forms.

I try to encourage the children to do a book report for every book they read since some forms are no more difficult than copying the book's title along with their own name. However, many children resist any form of written follow-up, so I usually set a minimum number of reports per semester and am satisfied to have the children do additional reading and discuss it with me or with their classmates. Over the years, I have devised many new reporting forms as new situations arose. Often the children's ideas have been incorporated into new forms. All the forms are kept in a file available to the children, who may select any one. The student is urged to try a variety of forms.

KEEPING THINGS ORDERLY

The teacher who is attempting individualization for the first time may wonder how to keep track of the whirlwind of activity in which she finds herself. And after all, as the teacher, you do have to know what's going on. You have to monitor the students' work, keep tabs on where they are and what they're doing during the day, find efficient ways of collecting and returning papers, and so forth. Here are some techniques which I have found very useful.

Work Contracts

A work contract is an agreement between the teacher and the child, outlining certain tasks which the child plans to accomplish in some specified length of time. There are probably as many different work contracts as there are teachers. In ten years of teaching I have experimented with over twenty adaptations of contracts I had seen other teachers use. The contracts you use must suit *your* specific goals and the needs of your students. Here are some samples of types of contracts I have found useful. (See Appendix B for samples of each of the work contracts discussed below.)

1 *Assigned tasks:* I select a list of assignments, which may be drawn from a single area or a variety of areas, and tell the children they are to be done by some specified time. The children then check off each task as they complete it and I initial each item as the work is checked. Actual scores may be recorded right on the contracts, which are then saved for help in evaluating the pupil at report time or during a parent conference. These shortcuts to record keeping can be done with all forms of contracts.

2 *Assigned areas:* This contract requires that the child do some work from each subject area daily. There is a list of teacher-selected choices in each area. For example, in math I might offer some of these choices: text pages, worksheets to drill on facts, measuring, telling time, work problems, speed tests on which the students time each other, manipulative chores such as making bundles of tens and hundreds, liquid or linear measuring, math games (checkers, chess, flash card contests), and so forth. All of these activities are completely run by the pupils. Students check off the tasks as they are finished. This contract may also be used on a weekly basis.

3 *Area contracts:* Here, a separate contract is used for each academic area. I may assign specific work or leave the choice up to the child. In general, I prefer a combination of both. When the choice is made, I paste the contract to a folder in which the student keeps all his work, so that when I collect the contracts I also have the student's finished work. This method is especially useful when it comes time to evaluate any specific area of work. As with all contracts, both the

student and I comment on the contract as tasks are completed and corrected. This helps me to see at a glance if the student is progressing according to his own abilities.

4   *Timed areas:* This type of contract requires that a specific minimum amount of time be spent in several areas. This type seems to work well with intermediate students who have had some chance to be self-directed and to work on an individual basis. Under the headings of the subject areas (which I have selected) there are blanks for the student to fill in what he has accomplished. I usually use this type of contract when I am concerned about the amount of work children are doing. It provides some structure for budgeting their time. Therefore, initially they have freedom only within the academic areas I have selected. If the children no longer need this structure, they may be free to select both the area of work and the time spent on it. This contract plan now becomes similar to the simpler Daily Log explained in number 7. The use of this form allows the teacher to be very specific, for the children who need more teacher direction, simply by filling in the exact work she expects the child to do. As the pupil becomes more self-directed he should be able to function nicely if left to determine his own specific tasks.

5   *Choice:* The children are presented with a list of as many as thirty tasks from all subject areas. Each child must do a major portion of *any* twenty of the given tasks by a specified date. Some of the tasks might include several compositions; varied art projects; listening to classical music; creating original crossword puzzles; choreographing a modern dance solo or duet; making a set of flashcards for math or vocabulary cards for reading; writing and acting out a play or puppet show; writing rules for a playground game; or straightening one's desk daily. I usually use this form of contract before a holiday. All those who complete the contract earn the right to come to a class party. Each task should be broad enough to allow for differing student abilities.

   The choice contract should be introduced as a fun project. I usually use this along with other more academic contracts or assignments. If this procedure proves successful, it can become the usual monthly routine. Some choice contracts offer rewards in the actual work (i.e., pride in a job well done) rather than external rewards, such as a party. I try to gear the tasks to the slower learner. I offer many fun activities where "learning" seems secondary to the child. For example, one choice contract asked for a colorful folder or paper woven basket for storing completed tasks, another for a pin with a happy slogan, and still another for an original set of flashcards or an original math game. The children had so much fun they did not realize that they were doing "school" work.

6   *Free schedule:* This contract provides a daily schedule. There are usually time blocks in half or whole hours for one day or one week. The child fills in his plans for the day, and evaluates his own achievements at the end of the day. He is asked to respond to questions such as "Were your goals realistic?" and "How much did you accomplish?" The children seem to find self-evaluation difficult (don't we all!) but begin to enjoy it as they get more experience in discovering why they were or were not successful. This type of contract is a commitment, on the part of the pupil, to set and improve his work habits.

7   *Daily logs:* After working on any one task the pupil has to record what he did in the proper time block. The daily log and accompanying work are collected at the end of the day for teacher evaluation. While I do some evaluating during the day, I usually wind up with lots of "homework" because it is important that these logs be returned to the students first thing the next morning if my comments are to have much meaning. I use a dittoed form giving half-hour time blocks in the left margin, followed by a long line for the children to write in what they have done. I fill in recess and lunch times but ask the students to account for every other block of time. There is a space at the bottom of the sheet for a daily self-evaluation. This form helps the children to evaluate their use of time. A daily log may be used with any one of the above contracts or in lieu of a contract.

Some children find security in receiving the same contract over and over again, while others are more stimulated by a change of contract forms. The teacher is the best judge of this. Be flexible. Experiment on your own.

Whether I am "pacing" (letting each child do the assigned tasks at his own rate) or individualizing (where the children select their own assignments based on personal interests), contracts help me to organize and keep fairly accurate tabs on all the pupils' progress.

Student Conferences

I have found conferences a valuable way of monitoring student progress. I try to have a conference with each child at least every other day. The purpose of the conference may be to have the child read for me or discuss a story; or it may be to review with the child all the work he has done since the last time we held a conference.

I keep a file box with an index card for each child. The card has two columns, showing date and comments about conferences held with the child. As the child comes to me for a conference, I make notes on recall, comprehension, or other reading skills; and at times I record comments concerning matters that require follow-up, such as "Next time, read a more difficult book," or "Prepare your social studies outline by tomorrow." These recorded comments are always read to the child.

I arrange conferences by listing five to seven student names on the board. While I am having a conference with the first child, the second child gets ready by gathering all work he will need for his conference.

The children are also given a chance to sign up for a conference if they feel the need to see me. For this purpose, I make the general heading "Conferences" on the board and let the children write their names if they wish any type of help, or I designate a particular area, such as "Conferences for Social Studies." This second method is often useful for providing temporary groups for short review lessons on specific topics.

I rarely use my chalkboard for teaching since most of my contact with students is on a one-to-one or small-group basis, but my board is always filled with the names of pupils I want to see and who want to see me. I love the personal touch to conferences. No more "front of the room" teaching for me. Through conferences, I am continuously learning with my students, and, more important, I truly enjoy being with them.

The Numbers Game

One great time-saving device for keeping tabs on what is happening in the classroom is the use of numbers. At the beginning of the year, I assign to each child a numbered mailbox. All of the boxes are arranged in alphabetical order. The number of the box then becomes that child's own number, which he uses for many different purposes. For example, as part of every heading, each child places his number in the upper-right-hand corner of his paper. This makes it very easy to alphabetize any collected written work. In addition, when I collect work I can easily note and record on the chalkboard those "numbers" whose papers are missing.

I also keep track of completed work by drawing boxes on the

chalkboard and labeling them by subject heading. As students complete an assignment they write their number in the proper box.

The numbers system is useful for taking attendance and for grouping children for games as well. When the morning bell rings the children automatically count off by number. A short silence between numbers means that a child is absent. For games, the children or I form teams by counting by threes or fours, by division into "odd" and "even," and so forth.

Sign-Out System

The children themselves are a very valuable resource in my attempts to keep track of what is happening in the classroom. I have found that reliance on them pays off in many ways. For example, by making the students responsible for signing themselves out when they leave the room, I am able both to keep track of their whereabouts and to allow the free flow of students to other areas of the school.

A more structured sign-out system requires the use of a 3×5 card for each child. The card is divided into areas where the children might want to roam, such as the library or lavatory. They fill in the date under the proper heading and pin the card to the bulletin board chart with the same heading. Upon returning, they cross out the date. This allows the teacher to tell at a glance how many children are in a given area at a given time, and it also allows her to keep tabs on how often a particular child leaves the room.

A freer method of pupil movement is possible with a chart indicating various student destinations—another room, learning center, office, library, lavatory, etc. Each child must have a name tag, and if a tag is lost it is the child's responsibility to make a replacement. The children keep their name tags pinned under the proper heading on a chart. The chart may be a simple, plain one, or both chart and tags may be related to a decorative theme, such as Christmas, Easter, or Valentine's Day.

Just keep hoping for no pupil-counting chores like fire drills when half the class is out of the room. . . .

Monitors

The children are also very useful and willing helpers in their role as monitors. Every two weeks we elect a president, vice-president, secretary, and treasurer. Their chores include taking the lunch count, leading the pledge, passing out notices, and tending the class library. *All other jobs are handled by the class Pet.* I go down my attendance list so every child gets his turn at being Pet. Each day we have a new Pet, who then selects a helper. The children love this and count the days until their name is next on the attendance sheet. Each child gets several turns during the school year. Between our president and his cabinet and our Pet and his assistant we have elected, appointed, and selected helpers. No one may run for a class office a second time until everyone has had one turn at each office. If we elect a boy president and runner-up vice-president, then we select a girl secretary and runner-up treasurer. The next semi-monthly election then calls for girl president candidates and boy secretary candidates.

KEEPING RECORDS

The children keep about 95 percent of all "my" records—charts and graphs of scores for specific subjects such as spelling, or scores of reading worksheets. All answers are made available to the children, and they usually correct their own or a peer's work. They enjoy using the teacher's manuals for this purpose. It seems to make them feel more important.

Index cards stapled to construction paper folders are great for recording scores, while larger cards, stapled to folders, are handy for recording the titles of books read by each child. The folders themselves contain corrected papers and book reports.

Folders and files are placed in decorated cartons or similar receptacles. (I strongly recommend the use of these, as opposed to letting the children keep things in their desks, where papers tend to get lost or bedraggled.) These are placed on any open space such as the tops of bookcases or window ledges, so that both the students and I have easy access to them.

I find that the children are very capable of keeping their own records, and that they value the opportunity to monitor themselves. And what a clerical relief for me! Spot-checking through conference records and orally reviewing a page with a child is more meaningful than spending hours at home correcting papers which will only be glanced at or lost by children. This plan also leaves me more time to prepare new work and to correct any tests that may be given.

SUMMING UP

My first year was very neatly organized individualization. All of the children had to do reading from nine to ten o'clock. Everyone had minimum requirements such as one book report weekly, assigned SRA power builders twice a week, text workbook pages daily, and compositions biweekly. The longer I individualize, the freer I am getting. Now I no longer have a specific reading time. The children still have minimum requirements, but they are not as rigid. Guidelines are given to the few who need more teacher direction.

Specific "mileposts" are, to a large extent, controlled by the subjective feelings of the teacher. Your tolerance of new situations and your own personality often give you more direction than any manual or I could do. New situations that may cause anxiety or feelings of insecurity should be faced in accordance with your own skills and aptitudes. How "free" you feel in working with a group of children is a highly individualized matter with no right or wrong. You must be comfortable with your class before they can be comfortable with you. If you truly believe in individualizing then you must believe in individual teacher styles and approaches to classroom situations, too.

After you get over your own fears of losing control of the classroom which may be caused by an increase in the noise level, the students' mobility, and those "problem" children who try to test you to see how much they can get away with, you are on your way to success. This usually takes *many* weeks; then you really begin to relax and thoroughly enjoy the children as they teach you how well they can function when given the chance to make some of their own decisions.

APPENDIX A: BOOK REPORTS

Following is a list of suggestions for making book reports. Each of these suggestions is presented on a book report form. The forms are filed by letter (Forms A through Z) and kept in a file with a sample booklet of forms in front of the file box. This method makes it easy for a child to leaf through the samples and select the forms that appeal to him.

Samples of a few of the forms which I have been using are also included.

Forty-nine Ways of Making Creative Book Reports

This compilation of suggestions for book reports is arranged in approximate order of difficulty.

1   Using modeling clay to depict a scene or characters from a book.

2   Making posters about a book, using paint, crayons, chalk, paper sculpture, ink, cut-out pictures, real materials.

3   Producing a "movie" of a book, creating a series of pictures on a long roll of paper or using pictures with a flip-book technique.

4   Creating a series of original illustrations for a story using any medium desired.

5   Using a flannel board, one child tells the story while another manipulates characters on the flannel board.

6   Dressing dolls to depict character(s) from a book.

7   Making sand table scenes or dioramas.

8   Telling a story to musical accompaniment.

9   Drawing a mural of the book.

10   Marking beautiful passages of description for oral reading.

11   Dramatizing a story: Several children may read the same story and can work together.

12   Describing orally or in writing an interesting character in a book to motivate other children to get acquainted with such a person.

13   Constructing a miniature stage, using pipe cleaner dolls.

14   Writing or telling the most humorous, exciting, interesting, sad, or pleasant incident in a book.

15   Writing a letter to a friend advising him to read a book.

16   Using information in the book to make a scrapbook about the subject.

17   Writing a simple book review for the school newspaper.

18   Pairing off for a conversation about a book.

19   Relating a significant incident or anecdote: Each student plays the role of a speaker on a TV program about good books.

20   Comparing two books on the same subject, two books on different subjects, or two books by the same author.

21   Making lists of new, unusual, or interesting words or expressions encountered in books read.

22   Sharing books about how to make or do things by having the readers give oral or written directions or demonstrations.

23   Writing one's own story from a book title; then, after having read the book, showing the class the difference in the two plots.

24   Reporting on a travel book, an illustrated lecture using postcards, magazine pictures.

25 Writing a series of questions which student thinks other readers should be able to answer after reading the book.

26 Giving a sales talk: The student represents himself as a salesman endeavoring to sell the book to the class.

27 Holding a round-table discussion chaired by a student: Four or five students read the same book and discuss it.

28 Producing a puppet show.

29 Giving a "chalk talk," using a cartooning technique.

30 Acting out a pantomime and encouraging the audience to guess what the story is about.

31 Making a critical analysis of a book.

32 Sharing books of poetry
   a   Choral reading
   b   Writing a composite poem
   c   Dramatizing poetry
   d   Collecting pictures to illustrate verses
   e   Accompanying poetry with various rhythmic activities
   f   Setting a verse to music
   g   Adding original stanzas to a poem (helps the children understand poetry construction and encourages them to write)

33 Reporting on a historical book by making a large pictorial time line or map.

34 Playing the role of a reporter at the scene: While it's happening, a crucial scene is described on the spot by a TV or radio reporter.

35 Decorating a book jacket and writing a blurb to accompany it.

36 Writing a movie script for a good action story (this experience helps children arrange events in sequence).

37 Holding an interview: A character in the book is interviewed by a reporter or by a TV interviewer. Other possibilities: A psychiatrist talks to a character who has psychological difficulties; a lawyer talks to a character who has legal difficulties.

38 Holding ceremonies for Recognition Day: Each student who has read a biography of a deserving person comes forward to make a presentation speech awarding a medal or citation.

39 Taking the role of the major character and, in a process of "thinking out loud," talking about the critical situation or problem he is facing at the high point of the story.

40 Writing an analysis from a specific standpoint: "A greater understanding of the problems people have to face and solve has come to me from the book _____ by _____."

41 Making a movie trailer or preview of coming attractions: Each student clips magazine or newspaper pictures—or sketches of his own—showing scenes similar to those of significant moments in his book.

42   Writing a letter in the role of a book character. The hero of *Lost Horizon* writes a letter about his final return to Shangri-La.

43   Writing or telling different endings to the story.

44   Writing a magazine ad for a book.

45   Holding an imaginary interview with an author or character in a book. One student can ask the questions of another who pretends to be the author or character.

46   Writing the diary of a major character. At least three crucial days in the life of the character are dealt with.

47   Giving a group performance, in the style of "This Is Your Life."

48   Doing a thirty-second or one-minute spot advertisement on radio or TV about a book or a character in a book.

49   Giving a monologue. Speaker assumes the character of a major figure in the book and describes his personality, his likes and dislikes, strengths and weaknesses, and enough of the typical situations in which he finds himself to make others want to read his "whole story."

FIGURE 3.1 SAMPLE BOOK REPORT FORM

My name is _____

This is my reading wheel.

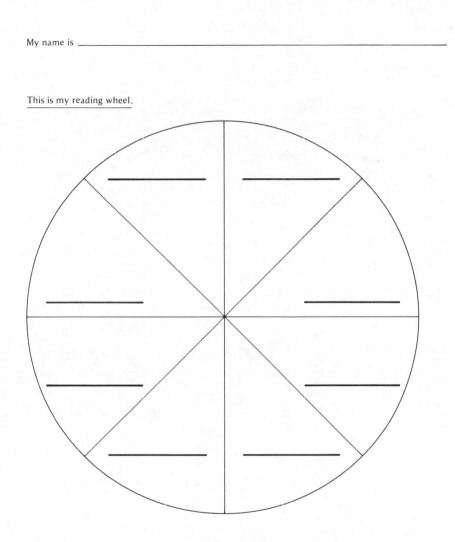

Good for primary grades. Children fill in categories of books on the lines. Categories may be agreed upon by class or they may be different for each child. Stars are pasted in each slice as a book is read in that category. Wheel is pasted on cover of book report folder.

FIGURE 3.2   SAMPLE BOOK REPORT FORM

My Selective Reading Program

For use with intermediate grades. Student puts dots, checks, or stars in each section as he reads a book in that area. Wheel is pasted on the front cover of student's book report folder.

FIGURE 3.3 SAMPLE BOOK REPORT FORM

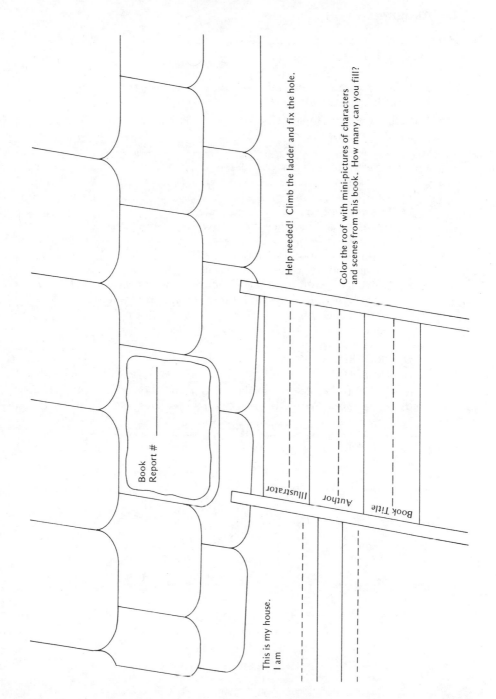

APPENDIX B: SAMPLE WORK CONTRACTS

1   Assigned Tasks

Name _____ May 10–22

Assignments

1   Math—separate sheet—fill in date when entire assign-   1 _____
    ment is completed

2   Social Studies—topic _____   2 _____
    List 2 references: _____

---

3   Language Arts—all tasks completed   3 _____
    A   Book report # _____ form _____   A _____
        Title _____
    B   Spelling test # _____   B _____
        words twice; sentences for 12 words, correct test   _____
    C   Letter to Rover or other pal   C _____
    D   Fictitious composition about "me"   D _____
    E   Nonfiction composition about "me"   E _____
    F   Dictionary work—use *Webster's New Practical*   F _____
        School Dictionary to find the meanings of these
        words. Use these words in sentences: "compli-
        ment" (p. 156), "ready" (p. 672), "heard" (p.____),
        "mystery" (p.____).
    G   Do 3 RFU   G _____
    H   Do 5 RT   H _____

4   Music—listen to Peter Tchaikovsky's *Piano Concerto*   4 _____
    #1 in B♭ Minor. What did it make you think about?

---

2 Assigned Areas

Fill in the date. Circle the day and date.

Monday   Tuesday   Wednesday   Thursday   Friday

_____ _____ _____ _____ _____

You must complete one task in every area every day. You may do more.

A Reading   Checked by teacher
   1 Read aloud to a teacher or helper.   _____
   2 Read aloud to a friend. p. _____ Name _____   _____
   3 Read silently, book _____ p. _____   _____
   4 Do a book report *(must finish book first)*.   _____
   5 Work on a S.S. Project _____ read _____ correct notes
      _____ take notes _____ do good copy   _____
   6 Other _____   _____

B Spelling (List _____)
   1 Write your words twice and put them into
      sentences.   _____
   2 Write a story using your spelling words.   _____
   3 Make up a crossword puzzle with your spelling
      words as the answers.   _____
   4 Find rhyming words for your words.   _____
   5 Make up your own list (10 words) and put the
      words into sentences.   _____
   6 Other _____   _____

C Math (Must do text work every day!)
              grade   grade   grade
   1 Text work p. _____ _____ p. _____ _____ p. _____ _____   _____
   2 Flash card drill with $\times \div + -$ (circle when done)   _____
   3 Number families or tables _____   _____
   4 Speed test on $\times \div + -$ monitor _____ grade _____   _____
   5 Other _____   _____

Evaluation: Today I _____

3   Area Contract

Name _____ January 4–8

Happy New Year Assignment Sheet

These tasks are to be completed by January 8 (this Friday). Be sure to fill in the date when you complete an assignment.

Date

Language Arts	
1 Book Report # _____ form _____	
Title: _____	1 _____
2 Spelling Test # _____	
Write each word twice. Put any dozen words in sentences.	2 _____
3 Do 2 RFU and 2 RT	3 _____
4 Math—Fill in the pages as you finish them—7 this week.	all 7 pages are done ↓
M _____ T _____ W _____ Th _____ F _____	4 _____
5 Compositions—one each	5 _____
A Nonfiction (true)	A ____
My Vacation	
Happy Holidays	
Welcome New Year	
B Fiction (make-believe)	B ____
Jack Frost	
Winter Wonderland	
Sam Snowflake	
6 Clean out your desk on Friday.	6 _____

4   Timed Area Contract

1   Reading—15 minutes (time limits may vary with different groups)
Book title _____
Pages read _____ to _____
Time* _____ : _____ to _____ : _____
2   Math—15 minutes
Book (only if there is a choice for pupils) _____
Pages done _____ to _____
Number of examples completed _____
Number of examples done correctly _____
3   Social Studies—10 minutes
Work done† _____

---

* (Optional—fits in nicely if studying telling time.)
† (Could be reading, note taking, other research, etc.)

NOTE: This sample is very sketchy because the time allowances and required work will vary so greatly with each task.

5   Choice Contract

Name _____ February 2–14

Party Contract

Here is a list of a dozen tasks. You are to select any 7 tasks. You must complete your seven tasks by noon on Monday if you wish to come to our Valentine Party on Monday at 1:00.

Circle the numeral by the task you do and have a teacher check your work right away. Try to complete one task every day.

Tasks	Teacher's comments
1 Make a Valentine box to hold your Valentines. It must be decorated.	1 _____
2 Write a special Valentine letter to your mom telling why you love her.	2 _____
3 Plan an original Valentine or February crossword puzzle. Be sure to give easy clues. Use the anagram letters to plan your puzzle. Copy your puzzle on paper.	3 _____
4 List 5 words for all the long and short vowel sounds. The words should be from different word families (like "day" and "bake").	4 _____
5 Plan a checkers tournament. Keep a list of all the players and make a graph or chart to show the results. You may play, too.	5 _____
6 Tell five facts about good dental health. How should you care for your teeth? Tell do's and don'ts.	6 _____
Are you thinking as you work? Smile! Work, work, work . . . Are you working your hardest?	
7 Write a true story explaining the story (superstition) of Groundhog Day.	7 _____
8 Measure our room and draw a room plan to the scale of $1'' = 1'$. Be sure to show the doors and windows.	8 _____
9 Keep a daily log for one day. Record the time and what you do.	9 _____
10 Read a library book to a friend or teacher. Name of Book _____ and friend.	10 _____
11 Draw a portrait of yourself or one of your teachers.	11 _____
12 Do a ditto worksheet from the box by the board.	12 _____

If the above tasks are too hard for you, you may substitute two from these easy chores. See the teacher for an "OK" first.

A Empty your mailbox and clean your desk.	A ____
B Do three job cards. _____ _____ _____	B ____
C Measure our room—use your own feet—and tell how many "feet" go each way.	C ____

6   Free Schedule

Name _____

Time Schedule

Fill in what you do and *when* you do it. Include conferences and games (Learning Center and being a helper). Got the idea? This is a *log*.

Monday
9– 9:45 _____
10–10:30 _____
11–12:05 _____
1– 1:45 _____
2– 3:15 _____
Today I was (a) poky (b) lazy (c) a good worker (d) so-so.

Tuesday
9– 9:45 _____
10–10:30 _____
11–12:05 _____
1– 1:45 _____
2– 3:15 _____
So far all of my work is (a) completed neatly (b) finished sloppily (c) almost done (d) incomplete.

Wednesday
9– 9:45 _____
10–10:30 _____
11–12:05 _____
1– 1:45 _____
2– 3:15 _____
Reminder: Talent Show → end of March → sign up!!

Thursday
9– 9:45 _____
10–10:30 _____
11–12:05 _____
1– 1:45 _____
2– 3:15 _____

Friday
9– 9:45 _____
10–10:30 _____
11–12:05 _____
The rest of today should be for fun group lessons.

7   Daily Log

Date_____

Name _____

On the line after each time, fill in what you did during that half hour. At the bottom of the sheet, circle the words that describe how you did today.

9:00– 9:30 _____

9:30–10:00 _____

10:00–10:30 _____
Recess

11:00–11:30 _____

11:30–12:00 _____
Lunch

1:00– 1:30 _____

1:30– 1:45 _____
Recess

2:00– 2:30 _____

2:30– 3:00 _____

Today I was (a) poky (b) lazy (c) a good worker (d) so-so.
My work today was (a) completed neatly (b) finished sloppily (c) almost done (d) incomplete.

CHAPTER 4

INDIVIDUALIZING FOR SLOW READERS

Carolyn Miller

This teacher's commitment to the teaching of basic reading skills led her to the adoption of a number of interesting strategies for individualizing. She is concerned with matching teaching methods with learning styles of individual students and with using a variety of assessment techniques to determine not only skill deficiencies, but the feelings of children about the experience of reading as well. Her eclecticism in choosing media other than books will be comforting to those who see limitations in many of the materials flooding the market.

The format of this chapter must of necessity be rather different from the ones that have preceded it. At present, I conduct a "pull-out" program in reading and mathematics for groups of from six to ten children who come to my mini-room (actually the school's old storeroom) because they are below expected grade-level performance. However, rather than focus any discussion on this particular experience, I prefer to draw on it as well as my previous years of teaching at all levels. What follows is a collection of ideas and experiences, particularly with slow learners, which I feel might have application in many other teaching situations. They are offered in the form of suggestions rather than as a description of what I do in a given year.

Four years ago, when I joined the staff of a school committed to trying new ideas in education, I was very excited. Here was the opportunity to try ideas which I was convinced would result in happier and more effective teaching and learning! At the same time, I was somewhat apprehensive. I questioned the wisdom of some of our current educational innovations. I had personal reservations about team teaching, for I wasn't convinced that this type of organization was necessarily best for primary-age children. I had some doubts about open education, in which children decided what and when they would learn. This seemed like an abdication of the school's responsibility to the child. My belief in the absolute necessity of each child developing basic reading skills and my previous course work in reading led me to question whether or not a completely open, free-choice oriented, individualized reading program was realistically efficient and able to provide the needed instruction in basic skill areas such as phonics. However, I was eager to learn and willing to change and grow.

Not all my questions are gone, nor have all my doubts disappeared. I have, however, eliminated some instructional alternatives as undesirable and/or unfeasible. I have also developed a firm commitment to the idea of individualizing instruction. I have been able to define it for myself in a meaningful, though general, way, and I have discovered and developed some teaching strategies that work for me.

To me, individualized learning in reading means that, to the greatest extent possible, each child develops his or her abilities and interests in reading. This individualized learning requires an atmosphere and an attitude conducive to learning and the conviction that every child and every teacher is an individual. No method or book provides the panacea for all teachers or students. Rather, individualized learning takes place in a classroom where there is warmth, happiness, laughter, and guidance, where the teacher believes in the children's ability to learn and in the effectiveness of his methods, and where the children respect each other and take pride in their achievements.

I have ruled out a variety of alternative approaches to teaching. First, we know that children mature at different rates and have different levels of ability, different experiential backgrounds, and different learning styles. It seems therefore both inefficient and irrational to teach the same lesson to all students at the same time and expect them all to learn. Second, it is equally inefficient and perhaps irrational to attempt to work with all students on a completely individualized daily tutorial program in every area. If you are a primary teacher who meets with a class of thirty students each day, you might be able to devote ten minutes to each child. Not very satisfactory! Thirdly, I have found that the traditional "three reading group" approach is inadequate. Within each group, there is still a very wide range in achievement and ability, and there are always those children who simply do not "fit" into any of the groups. I have found that even remedial reading students, who are all considerably below the expected grade level performance, differ in their particular skill strengths and weaknesses.

Some, for example, have a good sight vocabulary, but lack the ability to apply phonetic skills to identify a new word. Others become confused when words don't follow phonetic patterns and need to develop the ability to use context clues in reading. Just grouping children as slow, average, or fast readers is obviously not enough.

The solution which I have found most effective is to adapt the system to the children by grouping the children and individualizing within the groups. SRA Reading Kits, *Reader's Digest* Skill Builders, the Talking Alphabet, the Durrell-Murphy Phonics Program, Phonovisual materials, a variety of basic texts and library books, reading contracts with the children, and teacher and class-written stories and books are among some of the materials I have used to individualize within the reading program. I will elaborate on some of these later on. First, let me offer some suggestions for getting your reading program started.

GETTING STARTED

One can adapt ideas and techniques from a variety of programs. Success, it seems to me, depends greatly upon the teacher's use of his or her own teaching style and, if possible, matching children and teachers according to the child's learning style and the teacher's teaching methods. Each spring, teachers in our school describe the type of classroom organization they would like to use the following year. The child's current teacher fills out an index card indicating the type of classroom in which the child would probably be most successful and his achievement levels in various subject areas and then places the card in the envelope of a teacher who intends to have that particular plan of classroom organization. If, after two or three weeks of school, a child seems misplaced or a parent requests a change, the child is usually transferred to another room. Transfers are also made during the year as the need arises.

Arranging the Classroom

School is home to children during the day. For this reason, I think a cheerful classroom which encourages them to think, discover, learn, communicate, and work comfortably has an important effect upon their attitudes. A classroom, it seems to me, should reflect the philosophies and the interests of the students and the teacher.

The classroom diagram presented here (Figure 4.1) is a suggested arrangement for an air-conditioned classroom, thirty feet square, with no windows (the type of classroom currently used by most teachers in our school). Bulletin boards may be planned for any parts of the walls, as the walls are made of a material into which pins may be inserted.

Personally, I still feel more comfortable when each student has his own desk in which to keep things. If there isn't room for both desks and learning centers, I would suggest buying small dishpans or some other suitable type of storage containers and using or making shelves on which to store them. If such containers are provided, students can then use tables instead of desks for various activities. This arrangement leaves more floor space for learning centers. It is important, I believe, for each student to have the security of knowing where he can put things which he will need or want later.

A rug is essential. It enables me to have the class or a group meet quickly and provides a feeling of intimacy not possible when children are sitting at desks or tables. Students readily play their reading or math games on the rug and seem to enjoy sitting on the rug to read.

Completed worksheets which are to be turned in to the teacher may be placed in interlocking plastic vegetable bins stacked on the table next to door no. 1. These bins cost under a dollar and are usually available in supermarkets and variety stores.

I have found that distribution of worksheets to the correct groups is facilitated by putting them in construction paper folders of given colors and pinning the folders to the bulletin board. Thus, Group I's papers are always in green folders; Group II's in red, etc.

Legal-size file folders in a large cardboard box (covered with contact paper) help to keep those worksheets together. Students can place most of their finished, returned worksheets in these folders and then periodically staple the worksheets together and take them home. (However, I would keep representative samples to discuss with parents.)

Assessing the Children

I test children and then have a private conference with each student concerning his or her feelings toward reading. To simplify the testing process, I would suggest using the Wide Range Reading Achievement Test as a basis for determining additional tests which would be helpful in more accurately assessing the student's present strengths and weaknesses in reading. The Wide Range Achievement Test is administered

FIGURE.4.1   SUGGESTED CLASSROOM ARRANGEMENT

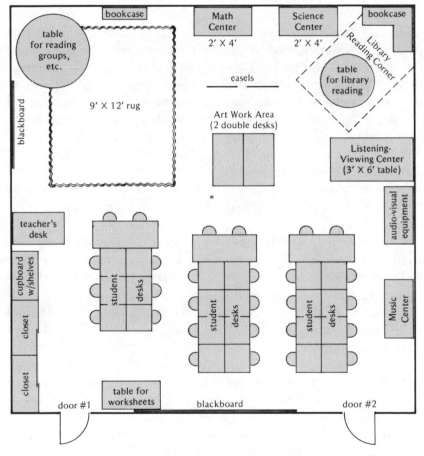

*Area in which to put additional student desks (adjust art work area if necessary).

individually, requires a minimum of time, has a range of pre-kinder-garten to twelfth grade, and offers two different word lists, one for children below the age of ten and another for those older than ten.

For children who score approximately 4.0 or below on the Wide Range, I would suggest the Durrell-Murphy Word Perception Test. This test is easily administered to a group or class and provides information on the child's phonetic word-attack skills.

The informal inventory requires more time and is administered individually but is extremely valuable because it provides information on the child's sight vocabulary, comprehension, and oral reading at all levels. Although my school district now has informal inventories for the three basic series used in elementary programs in California, a teacher can develop his own informal inventory for the book or books he expects to be using. Essentially, the teacher makes a list of at least twenty new words from a place near the middle of the book. When a child misses two words out of the list, he is given a selection of 100 running words, also from near the middle of the same book. The student is at the correct instructional level if he misses no more than five of the 100 words and can answer correctly five comprehension questions.

A teacher may find it necessary to give the student an informal inventory from a less or a more difficult book, depending upon the child's performance. However, the Wide Range provides an indication of the informal inventory level which is probably appropriate for a given student. Publishers' tests which accompany texts and workbooks and the starter stories in SRA kits may also be used to assess students' levels in reading.

When I confer with the students individually, I not only explore *their* feelings about reading, but I also tell them mine. I explain to them what their test scores show me about their reading abilities and give them some indication of my expectations.

For example, when I asked one sixth grade boy if he could give me the short sound of "i" and he couldn't, I showed him the word "finger" and told him he had misidentified the word on a test. I then explained how knowledge of the short "i" sound would have helped him to identify the word correctly. He tried reading a few short words such as "fit," "sit," "bill," and "pin." Since he could then sound these words out, we returned to the word "finger." A conference such as this not only helps me to learn more about the student, but it also provides my first real opportunity to work with him on a one-to-one basis and to show him he can learn. *A positive approach is a wonderful experience for a child!*

It is important for the teacher to truly appreciate the fact that reading can be fun but that learning to read usually involves a great deal of effort. Surely anyone who has tried to learn a new language in a foreign country has experienced frustration, and learning a language in a class requires a great amount of concentration. Yet, even though learning to read might be a formidable task for some children, they must be convinced *early* that they can do it. Children, I think, really appreciate it when you exhibit confidence in them. Tell them it will be a challenging task, but also tell them that they are capable of doing it. Through these conferences, you can convey your attitude and lay the groundwork for a good rapport between the teacher and students.

Beginning the Program

I spend a considerable amount of time during the first weeks testing, diagnosing, having conferences, and organizing, but, at the same time, I do want the students to be reading from the beginning of the year. So, before school opens, I place a variety of supplementary readers on the bookshelves. These are usually borrowed from the central district library in sets of five to ten each. (Of course, there are many library books besides.) If you don't have these books available, I would suggest checking book fairs at public libraries for good bargains in used books. Swap meets and flea markets are other potential sources of inexpensive books. Invest in paperbacks.

As I've indicated earlier, I believe that children are basically very reasonable and respond positively when they are given logical explanations for following certain procedures. Therefore, I explain that it will take a while for the testing and conferences, but, in the meantime, they'll have an opportunity to select books to read by themselves. Taking about half of the class at a time, I show them some of the books (easy, medium, and difficult) and, frankly, become a book salesman. Generally I've arranged the books so that those of similar difficulty are in the same area.

My aim is to encourage the children to read a story or book, regardless of how easy it may be. It has been my observation that children usually select books with which they are comfortable. Sometimes, of course, a poor reader will try difficult books in order to maintain the respect of his peers. However, I tell the children they are free to

exchange the book if it's really too hard or too easy or they don't enjoy it. Be careful here! Some limits have to be set. Ordinarily I say,
"You may try one or several books today; however, by Thursday
[Thursday being the day after tomorrow] I expect you to begin reading
at least one book you like." Have the children go to the library in
small groups at first; otherwise there may be pandemonium. On the
day designated for a choice of book, have the children write down the
name of the book which they are reading.

If a student does persist in selecting books that are too difficult,
find three or four that are easier and ask him if he would help you by
looking them over and telling you which one he would recommend
for another student. From the beginning, convey the idea that the
child's opinion is important. We, as adults, can't always accurately predict what they will like.

During these first few weeks, then, I set aside at least half an hour
a day for this independent reading. For the first three or four days of
this reading, I don't try to test during this hour. Instead, I just move
from one student to another, observing, asking about the book, and
listening to them read a sentence, a paragraph, or a page. About once a
week I ask the children to make up three to five questions and answers
about what they've read.

By the second week of school I can usually identify the best readers in the class. Then I ask some of them to take turns being a
"Teacher Assistant" for a day. Children who need help with words can
then go to the assistant or assistants assigned for the day and I am
free to test and to have conferences. I find having two or three assistants each day is better than having only one. This prevents children
from waiting for help and offers the child a choice if he is reluctant to
ask a particular child for help. After the regular reading program is
under way, we continue to have assistants both in reading and in math.

Since the ability to read and follow directions is so vital to academic success, I usually begin teaching direction words and phrases
such as "underline," "encircle," "draw a line," etc., at the very beginning of the year. This instruction is particularly appropriate for fourth
graders and for below-average fifth and sixth graders. Students can
then do appropriate worksheets independently while I test.

Set aside a time for individual independent work in math, writing,
art, and the independent reading period. During this time you are
working with a student (testing, holding conferences, etc.) and are not

to be disturbed. That time belongs to the student with whom you are working. (We discuss this as a class.) Also, some children need to learn to skip problems or items which they don't understand, to do what they can, and then to ask for help.

Grouping and Individualization

I group the students into three or possibly four groups for reading. This grouping is based upon an overall view of the children's test results and my observations of them. For example, the lowest group might know consonant sounds, blends, and a few short vowels and be able to read a primer or a first grade reader. The high group may have the greatest range, with one or two being considerably ahead of the others. The extreme lows and highs will be the first to work in more individualized programs.

To me, the grouping is a means to an end. It allows me to work with a relatively small group, provides a basis for scheduling different activities for the groups, and gives children the opportunity to discuss what they have read. It seems to me that one of the problems with better readers is their need to improve in reading comprehension. Often comprehension is hindered by failure to understand concepts or vocabulary. Group discussion and visual aids can help considerably in developing children's concepts.

The groups are very flexible. If children are between groups, I may have them read with two groups and not require follow-up assignments. Or they may read with a more advanced group and do assignments for the lower group. I simply say, "This week [or today, or for a while] let's have Mary and John read with Tom's group as well as their own." I may just tell the student he doesn't have to do the written assignment, but I would like for him to stay and read with the other group. If a child knows the skill involved in follow-up activities, he may have free time or be given another assignment instead. Children are changed from group to group whenever needed.

As much as possible, I avoid using the same series of books with different reading groups. With use of the same books for all groups, it is easy to associate the best readers with the group that finishes the books first. Each group generally has a supplementary book in which the students work independently, but they do have a certain minimum assignment to do daily or weekly.

To avoid the stigma of a child's being in a low group, I try to place a great emphasis on the other talents of the low readers. Again, I think students sense and appreciate honesty. An atmosphere which conveys a feeling of acceptance, an expectancy that students will do their best, and a valuing of each person are essential for happy and effective teaching and learning. I've found that using some of the materials and techniques I will be speaking of helps to emphasize what the students are doing and not necessarily what they can read.

I have the students select a reading partner from within their reading group. Less advanced readers may then spend part of their time reading orally together; more advanced readers may have assignments which they discuss and do as a team. Having partners of similar ability prevents the less advanced student from sliding along. I ask the partners to agree on the supplemental reader they will use. This facilitates partner reading and still allows a variety of supplemental readers within any given group.

For the lowest group I give basic skill instruction and review daily. A written exercise, game, filmstrip, tape-recording, or similar activity is used as a follow-up after the students have returned to their seats. The group usually uses the same basic text when reading with me.

Generally, I meet with every group each day, Monday through Friday. However, the amount of time spent with any given group may vary. The groups usually meet on a regular schedule, with the low group meeting first, the middle group next, and the most advanced group last. I allow about fifteen minutes a day at the end of the period for free activities—games, library reading, "catching up." During this time I may hold a conference with a group or an individual or check library reading. Approximately an hour and a half is allotted to reading and reading-related activities.

Fridays are reserved for literature appreciation with the class as a whole, book reports (optional, and in such forms as "television shows" and dramatic presentations), conferences, and planning for the following week. This arrangement also allows extra time for library reading.

Initially, when children are first grouped and given assignments, I make the work relatively easy to complete within the daily period. The basic understanding is that work must be finished within the allotted time. (Exceptions are made frequently, but these are mutual decisions between the students and me.)

Once everyone realizes the importance of completing assignments, policies are established for groups and individuals. This is done in a conference situation. Students reading in different supplemental readers or using workbooks then know how much is expected of them over a week's period. Minimum standards for less independent students may be on a daily basis. For example, a group working in SRA may be required to complete a story a day.

In talking with a student I might say, "You've done a fine job this week. How many pages do you think you can do next week?" If it is near the end of the month and he's trying to meet a library reading contract, we may shorten other assignments. It really comes down to planning with the student. One fifth grade boy did no written reading assignments for a month, but instead spent all of his extra time reading and rereading two favorite books.

Some students may be working on a project in another subject and want to devote more time to it. Fine! Then they meet with their reading group for needed instruction in basic skills but may spend the remainder of the period on the other project.

RUNNING THE PROGRAM

Once the children have been placed in their reading groups and the classroom has become somewhat normal, we can move into our regular reading activities.

Diversifying Reading Activities

You cannot expect children to do all their learning from books. Students learn to read in many ways, and we teachers have to try a lot of different approaches. Here are some that I have found successful.

Students are very responsive to games such as Phonics Rummy, Grab, and Bingo. You can ditto the format for Bingo games and let the children develop lists of words using a particular phonetic sound such as short "a," and then fill in the Bingo cards themselves. Students who develop such a game can teach a small group of other children to play it.

For one reading group, I took many of the words from the local newspaper. Every week I gave the older students a list of advanced words to be studied. The students were expected to be able to read and use these words by the end of the week. I included definitions of the words and used the words in sentences on the study sheet which the student received. Ordinarily, my practice would be to require students to look up the definitions, but the major objective of using these lists was to build the students' confidence and to enable them to have the experience of being able to read and use more sophisticated words. Less capable readers were required to learn a smaller number of words, perhaps the first five.

For those students who are somewhat slower in learning to read, I have used the following techniques. Students who need special help in phonetic skills use the Durell-Murphy Phonics Program, which enables them to work individually and to check their own work. I make large class-size vocabulary and phonetic vocabulary flash cards and duplicate miniature flash cards for the students. (Rule the master off into sections; type or write in the words.) The students cut them apart and then study them at school and at home. Partners practice together. Students within a group have contests to see who can read the most words correctly by the end of a week or month. The children seem to enjoy competition with others of similar ability. Charts listing the names of students in a group and the skills to be learned are made. When the student can successfully read the flashcards of a particular skill set (such as the set of cards with long "a" and silent "e"), he receives a dot or check mark under that column. A certain number of dots or check marks earns a prize. Sets of worksheets involving specific skills, such as the use of suffixes or prefixes, are placed in folders labeled in accordance with the skills on the chart. When a student has completed this set of worksheets, I spot check to be certain he has mastered the skill and then I mark the chart. (This checking is done on Friday or during the fifteen-minute free period.) Students who want to talk to me list their names on the board so I know who needs testing or a special conference. I have at least a very short conference with every student at least once a week. I list the names of students I want to see on the board.

I also use books with high interest, easy vocabulary, and *small* print with the remedial upper grade students. (Boys and girls readily label a book with large print as too easy.) If such books aren't available, rewrite short stories and type them on ditto masters. Put the duplicated stories in construction paper books. Another possibility is to have the students dictate stories, and make individual books containing the stories of all students in one class (including the name of the author who dictated the story), cut up old books, take out pictures which show young children, and make small booklets of one, two, or several stories.

Students' interests and ideas can provide the springboard for strong motivation among a class. Sports cars took first place with my groups one year. A book and record on drag racing, which is part of a series of books and records geared to the interests of older students, was the most popular item in the section of the program concerned with sports cars.

Girls (and many boys as well) are very responsive to reading and learning to follow simple recipes, such as those for making pudding, jello, and butter. The recipes can be duplicated, put in booklets, and illustrated by the students.

Reading various common signs such as "exit," "for rent," "sale," "slow, school crossing," etc., is a valuable experience and provides children with reading skills which they can use immediately.

Keeping Track of What They Do

It is important for me, for the child, and for his parents that I keep records of what each student is doing. I need this information to help him progress and to keep his parents informed.

Contracts   I find that individual contracts for library reading are very effective. At the beginning of the month, each child determines how many library books he will read during that month. To encourage children to read longer books, fifty pages count as a book. I also set a minimum for some or all of the children. Naturally, a few children overestimate the number of books they will read, but after one or two months contracts become very realistic. No written reports are required. A child places the book he has read in a particular place in the room and I spot check his reading. Each child is asked to read several paragraphs or a page or two from the book and sometimes to tell briefly about the story. Usually there is at least a fifteen-minute library reading period during the language arts block, with about a half an hour on Fridays as a "free reading period." Every child who completes his contract for the month receives as an award a certificate in a construction paper frame. The form for the certificate is duplicated and large gold seals and colored ribbon are purchased from a local stationery store.

The contract can be a very simple form such as this:

Library Reading Contract

_____ promises to read _____ library

books during the month of _____.

Signed _____   _____

  Student   Teacher

I record the number of books and return the contract to the child. He keeps it in a folder with a list of the titles of the books he has already read and the number of pages he read in each book. He also keeps any written book reports in this folder.

Student Record Keeping In order to enable the students to progress at their own individual rates, I provide each student with a composition book in which he records his answers and I write comments and make future assignments. For supplemental reading books which have appropriate questions and skill exercises, I select the sections which will be of particular benefit to the children. I list these on a ditto master and then staple a copy of the list inside the composition book. If a child doesn't need the practice of a given skill, I simply note "omit" beside that particular item on his assignment sheet. I have found the _Reader's Digest_ Skill Builders and the _Tom Morgan Mystery Series_ especially helpful for this type of program. I review the students' notebooks at least once a week. Students working in the SRA Program keep all of their own records; however, I pull the answer card once a week and correct that day's work myself.

If a student is weak in specific word attack areas, such as using short vowel sounds or long vowel principles, I list these in his notebook (and on an index card for myself). As he masters these skills, he crosses them off. I have a handy, easy-to-check record for myself.

Our district has developed a reading profile which is a written record of the student's individual progress on the continuum of skills as outlined in the district guidelines for reading. The tests which accompany this profile are very helpful ways to check specific skills which I have taught. I give these to a group of children when I think they have mastered the skill. (Use of the tests is not mandatory.)

SOME CONCLUDING THOUGHTS

Turning from specific suggestions to some closing thoughts, I would like to emphasize my view of individualizing learning as a process— both for the teacher and for the students. At times, the changes involved can be very trying, especially for the teacher.

Research, discussion, and revision are constant components of the individualization process. I have read; talked with teachers, students, and parents; tried ideas, revised them, and tried again; and I am still changing.

I hope that you who read this chapter will respond to its spirit and will try those ideas which you consider appropriate for your circumstances. Above all, let's keep in mind our purpose: To focus education on the child as an individual.

CHAPTER 5

LIFE IN A
RESOURCE ROOM

Betty Reetzke

The joy and excitement of providing children with myriad discovery opportunities shines through this teacher's account of four
years in a Resource Room. While a Resource Room is a special
place which not all schools enjoy, any teacher can find in this
chapter a great variety of suggestions for providing free-choice
activities for children and for enriching his own life by creating
opportunities "to share, and to care . . . to talk to the children and
to be friends with them."

My teaching situation is a little different from the usual one. As a
regular teacher in a primary (K-3) school, I am in charge of the Resource or Discovery Room. Because this is my regular assignment, no
teacher on our staff has had to take more children than usual to free
me to work in the Resource Room. I also have a full-time paid aide.
Together with the children, we explore, discover, and grow.

It should be emphasized that the Resource Room is for *every*
child in the school: low achievers, high achievers, gifted, advantaged,
disadvantaged, and all the nice, sweet, little middle-of-the-road average kids, for whom there is never a special program. I never know
exactly who is going to come to my room on a given day. Each teacher
decides whom she will send and when. Most of the teachers use some
type of a rotation system for sending their children. However, it has
been stressed repeatedly, especially by the principal, that every child
is to be allowed to come on a regular basis. No child is to be deprived
because of misbehavior or failure to complete his work. On the other
hand, children are not to be sent just because they do finish their work
or please the teacher. We feel that, even if a child misses his math or
reading time once in a while when coming to the Resource Room, it

does not really matter. The program is supposed to be a supplement to classroom activities.

In the Resource Room, it is my purpose to give each child the opportunity to go as far as he wishes. I want each child to reach toward the ultimate of his potential. To do this, it is essential that I consider his individual needs. How is he like or different from the other children? What are his strengths and weaknesses? What background does he have that I can build upon and likewise encourage him to build upon? How can I turn on his "discovery" mechanism? What causes him to "turn off"? Each child needs to be unlocked or opened up—to be freed.

I begin working toward this objective by trying to provide a rich environment which will stimulate the child and involve his feelings, imagination, and capabilities. If I can help a child to become immersed in some aspect of his environment, to assume responsibility for what he does, and to evaluate his activities, the Resource Room more than justifies its existence. I will be helping children develop that capacity for self-direction so essential for success in individualized learning experiences. In Appendix A, I have included a brief statement about the goals and general operation of the Resource Room. This document, which is available to interested parents and visitors to the school, provides a skeleton outline of the program.

WHAT HAPPENS IN THE RESOURCE ROOM

Materials

I should tell you right away that other than my salary, there is no budget for this program. We have furniture that is not needed elsewhere; materials scrounged, begged, and borrowed (some science items from the high schools, for example); and donations from parents, teachers, and the PTA. I spend my own money on the program as well.

I send a letter to parents, providing a list of the sorts of things they might provide (see Appendix B). What we can't get from them, we frequently find in the alleys and back streets of Los Angeles. Collecting from the refuse bins of small manufacturing concerns is a wonderful way to acquire a supply of needed materials. Almost anything can become a valuable resource in this room.

As a result of our collection efforts, the room is filled with various activities and supplies which are available to the children every day. These include such things as construction and woodworking materials; animals to observe or handle—a rat, a rabbit, mice, turtles, a tortoise, a snake, a lizard, a toad, tropical fish, a sea life tank; a cardboard house and tent for play; games and puzzles; sand, clay, and various modeling materials; water in a large plastic tub to float objects and boats or to use for measuring; sewing equipment; clothing for dress-up play and make-believe; records, filmstrips, and tape recorder; typewriters; a little grocery store; plastic animals and people; books; shelves and tables with items to look at and explore, such as rocks, shells, prisms, mirrors, brainteasers, birds' nests; things children bring from home; art projects and easels for painting, and so forth.

We also have a math center containing scales, various measuring devices, an adding machine, geo-boards, manipulative devices such as pegs, blocks, a balance, a number line, tiles for counting, and other odds and ends which come and go. The science corner contains a good but simple microscope, a bioscope, hand lenses, bug cases, and materials for an area of interest that we are exploring, such as mealworms, color solutions, electricity, air, water, heat, and so forth. Sometimes it's seeds for planting; at other times it's simple inquiry materials such as the pulse glass, the ball and ring, the dunking bird.

Such things are always available for the children to use or to explore. On certain days of the week, there are special activities such as cooking (we make butter, breads, cookies, scrambled eggs, ice cream, soup, etc.); art projects which involve guidance (tie-dye, sand candles, collages, junk pictures, wood and shell objects); films; and animal talks. Figure 5.1 shows an example of the arrangement of the room. It is only an example, as the arrangement changes often, depending upon our needs.

Activities

In such a rich environment, there is almost no end to the projects and activities which we can pursue. While it is impossible to convey their variety, let me share with you just a few of them.

Ecology We emphasize ecology and try to gather and use scrap materials and things that might help fight pollution. For example, we collected the styrofoam trays on which our school lunches are served, cleaned them, and used them for many projects. We built things out of

FIGURE 5.1 RESOURCE ROOM ARRANGEMENT

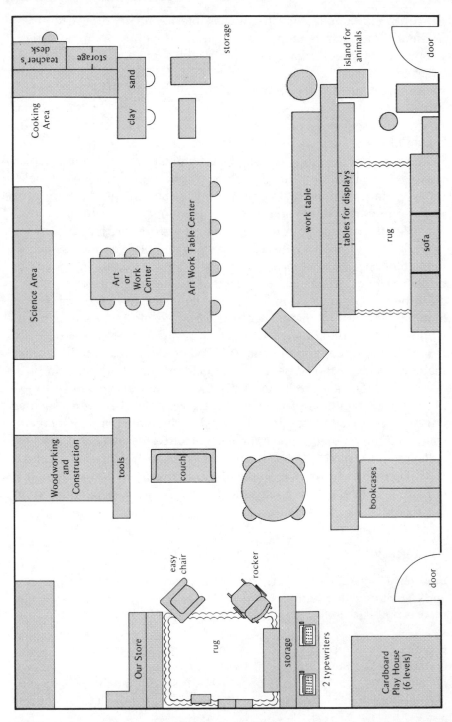

them, stitched designs onto them, dipped them in paint, and used them to print with.

Animal Study We weigh and measure all the animals, and keep charts of their growth. We have tried to train the animals and have timed the mice with a stopwatch as they ran through our wooden maze. Not only do activities like these reinforce learning which is taking place in the regular classrooms, but they also serve as the "take-off" point from which children can explore new avenues possibly not open to them in their own rooms.

Art We have loaded a table in the room with all sorts of "junk" and a sign saying, "What can you make?"

Paleontology We have some books and pictures about prehistoric times, as well as several examples of real fossils in the room. Many children seem to be interested in this period and particularly in dinosaurs. Sometimes we sit down in a group and just start talking. "Who has seen something like this fossil? What does it look like?" "Oh, it looks like the print of a seashell," or "This looks like a bug got stuck in the mud." If the children still seem interested, I show them some liquid rubber molds of simple fossils and allow them to make some by pouring plaster of paris into the molds. When the models have hardened, we paint them with water colors so that they look ancient. Then I give the children notes to take back to their rooms, telling what they've done and asking the teacher or parent to let them continue research along this line, if they wish.

Physics We have done a number of small experiments about air, using a plastic cup, test tube, a plastic tube ten inches long, and a soda straw. Before a child left the circle, he had to help another get started on the experiments.

HOW WE KEEP IT GOING

Organization

As you might imagine, the problems of scheduling and monitoring the movement of children in and out of the Resource Room can be considerable. Last year, we had a free-wheeling, "open-door" policy in the mornings, while the afternoons were set aside for the various clubs (e.g., science, poetry, photography, story time). However, due to organizational changes in the school as well as an increased desire on the part of teachers to have more time in which to send individual children to the room, a new scheduling procedure has evolved.

Each teacher is given a schedule to post in her room (see Figure 5.2). The schedule is large and has a colored dot to indicate each day in the week when the teacher can send her children to the Resource Room. In addition, each classroom is given three "special times" per week to visit the room. The special times are determined by the number of the group to which a teacher belongs. The groups are made up of teachers who team together and whose children eat lunch together. During these special times, a teacher may send at least four children to the room. If some of them leave during the hour, others can come in their place. Besides these special times, there are numerous "free times," when any teacher may send one child at a time. During these free times, we may have twenty to thirty children in the room. While we would like to increase the number of opportunities for visiting the Resource Room, this is presently impossible, since our school has more than nine hundred children in thirty classrooms.

When children come to the Resource Room, they wear a small cardboard clock suspended on yarn around their necks. (We have fastened the clock between two plastic coffee can lids for protection.) The classroom teacher sets the clock for the time that they leave their room. We can quickly look at the clock, and, after a certain period of time, depending on what project the children are working with, we send them back. Usually, another child immediately puts on the clock and comes. As I said before, most of the children come as a result of a rotation system; or, in some classrooms, they may choose the Resource Room as part of their free choice or free time activity. If the teachers use our schedule, children are able to come about every ten to twelve days.

Once in a while, the Resource Room becomes so crowded that we can't be at all effective. I feel that a group of twelve to fifteen children is ideal, but of course, for the sake of other staff members, I have to be certain that I have enough children each day! If we get too crowded, we put a sign on the door, "Closed until 9:15." The children who are arriving simply return to their own rooms and in the meantime we clear some out. We have only had to do this a few times, as the paper clocks help us to keep pretty good track of the children.

FIGURE 5.2 RESOURCE ROOM SCHEDULE

Monday	Tuesday	Wednesday	Thursday	Friday
8:30–9:30	8:30–9:00	8:30–9:30	8:30–9:30	8:30–9:30
Tinder Group #4 Grissom Monson Markarian Horst Levy	Reed Doss #1 Montgomery May	Flinchbaugh #5 Sweeney Crew Malis Sanders	Moore #3 Lites Allen Anderson Dolbec Restaino	Robinson #3 Whittinghill Warner Crossley Gram Williams
9:30–10:30	9:00–9:30	9:30–10:30	9:30–10:30	9:30–10:00
Free Science	Free	Free Art	Flinchbaugh #5 Sweeney Sanders Malis Crew	Reed May #1 Doss Montgomery
10:30–11:30	9:30–10:30	10:30–11:30	10:30–12:00	10:00–10:30
Free Special Things Cooking, Poetry Films, Crafts	Moore #3 Lites Allen Anderson Dolbec Restaino	Free Special Things Poetry, Cooking Crafts, Films	Free Science	Free
12:30–1:30	10:30–12:00	12:30–1:30	1:00–1:30	10:30–12:00
Flinchbaugh #5 Sweeney Sanders Malis Crew	Free Science	Free Special Things or Whole Class (sign up)	Bounds #6 Martin Willis Fortlage	Free
1:30–2:00	1:00–1:30	1:30–2:00	1:30–2:00	1:00–1:30
Robinson #2 Whittinghill Warner Gram Crossley Williams	Robinson #2 Whittinghill Warner Crossley Gram Williams	Tinder #4 Monson Horst Grissom Levy	Moore #3 Lites Allen Anderson Dolbec Restaino	Tinder #4 Monson Grissom Horst Markarian Levy
	1:30–2:00			1:30–2:00
	Bounds #6 Martin Willis Fortlage			

Within the Resource Room, the children choose what they want to do. Making decisions is an important activity in this room. However, we guide or help those who have problems making choices. If they would prefer to just sit in the rocking chair and rock or at times just observe, that, too, is fine. Children learn in different ways. But if they do decide to get involved in some activity they are expected to be responsible for the care and use of equipment and materials. They are expected to respect and to be kind, gentle, and considerate to animals. If they start a project involving art supplies or wood, we do expect them to complete it and not to waste things. Otherwise, the children are free to move from one activity to another during their allotted time. If they need to complete something after their time is up, we allow them to stay longer (with permission from their teacher) or we give them a note for a special appointment. When there are too many children at one activity, we usually let the first-comers continue and guide the extras to something else. Some areas have signs saying, "Three Only," or "You and One Friend."

Involving Parents

The parents also help us to keep the Resource Room going. Some of them give us help as volunteer aides. Last year, I had three excellent volunteers plus my paid aide. This year I have only one on a semi-regular basis. We struggle along. However, our parents are helpful in providing materials such as egg cartons, materials for sewing, empty boxes, bottles, etc. Sometimes I send a flier home with the children, but most of our donations come unsolicited from parents who want to help.

Problems

Of course, we do have some problems. We have some difficulty insuring that machines are properly used and adequately cared for although we're working on it. We try to watch when the children go to a machine and then try to assist them, if possible. We attempted to train the children to use the various machines and wrote their names in a notebook which was kept near the machines. If a child's name was listed, supposedly he had been trained and could use the machines without supervision. But we found it didn't work, for we never caught up. There were always names not in the book.

Now we have a few simple guidelines that have exceptions. Usually, if a child at least knows his letters and his numbers, he may use the typewriter or adding machine with one finger. If a child breaks the rules, he is asked to leave the area and to do something else.

We also have some difficulty keeping the room clean. We encourage the children to clean up and put away their work. Even though we really work on neatness and orderliness, with so many children coming and going we have a certain amount of cleanup each day. However, we do have many plastic ice cream containers and cheese boxes which are labeled for various materials and the children soon learn where to put things.

Evaluation

Then, of course, there is the question of evaluation. Recently, some teachers visiting from outside the district wanted to know how we evaluate each child's performance and provide feedback to the teacher. I had to admit that I wasn't too concerned about this matter. I look for patterns, asking, "Are the children capable of choosing, making decisions, being responsible, getting along with others?" I exchange observations with teachers and talk with children about their accomplishments and their feelings and desires in terms of the Resource Room. To get feedback and suggestions from the whole school, I periodically send a form to each of the classrooms to survey student reaction to the room (see Appendix C). The main complaint from children seems to be that they don't get to come to our room as often as they wish.

In my role as teacher in a Resource Room, I am sometimes able to discover dimensions of a child that are not quite so evident in the regular classroom situation. Recently, I became very aware that one of our "culturally disadvantaged" children should be tested for possible giftedness. He speaks only a little English but is learning very quickly. After observing his long attention span while he worked with Tangrams and Mirror Cards and his unusual creative ability with art materials, I suggested to the teacher and principal that he be tested. Despite a language barrier, my suspicions were confirmed. While my "discoveries" are rarely so dramatic, I have been able to assist teachers with insights and information about children in their classroom.

I can truly say that I have seen many children make marvelous growth in the ability to make decisions for themselves and then carry through with them. In several cases, when I have mentioned this to the classroom teacher, I have found that we're in agreement.

For example, there is Larry. Last year, he would come in, rushing loudly from one thing to the next. He would start things and walk away, get upset if we insisted that he finish and not waste. But he began to make a little progress. Two weeks ago, I observed that he stayed in the construction corner for thirteen minutes. This past week, while using wood scraps, Larry worked for approximately thirty minutes and produced a fantastic pair of bookends. We were thrilled and so was he. The only thing is that he doesn't want to leave them for Open House. He also completed a game of checkers this week. This is a completely new pattern for him.

Then there is Marilyn. Her homeroom (third grade) was the Opportunity Room (for "problem" children), because no one would have her. The teacher in the Opportunity Room usually sent her to the Resource Room once a week. At first, she caused trouble with other children. I sent her out once when she refused to cooperate. She was very angry, but I told her that in order to come and stay she had to play by a few simple rules. From then on, I can honestly say that she behaved very well and we found that she was an outstanding little artist.

Dana was another jumping jack. Of course, his progress is also due to a fine, understanding male teacher. Sometimes he would literally go wild in my room. Today, he played the tone bells for five minutes and he can pick out several tunes. He sat at the big work table and used the pulse glass for at least five minutes. He mixed color solutions for ten minutes, even though he spilled a lot because he wouldn't keep the bottles on the tray. He didn't want to clean up the mess, but he did. Then he sat in the rocker and let the gray mouse crawl up and down his arm. He seemed almost angelic, quietly observing it.

Parents tell me that the children come home and try things or want to make items the same as we made in the Resource Room. Recently, Margaret's mother told me that they didn't have any drinking glasses to use on the table because Margaret had been working at filling glasses, beating on them with spoons, and making various tunes and scales as we had been doing.

Many of the children are developing their own ideas. One is making his own set of slides for the microscope. One has started his own chart of the weight of the rabbit, mice, and rat.

We seldom find a child now who just wanders. Most of them come and almost immediately find something to do. I've found some really good checker players among them. They get involved and talk back and forth, usually about the things they are doing. Dressing in old clothes is a favorite among the older girls. They really make believe and I'm certain some of them seldom get to do this. The boys, even the older ones, love the various hats and wear them around while they do other things. I think they miss that from kindergarten. For the most part, whatever they do, we can say, "Fine, if that's what you want. It's your decision."

Parents, community, and other schools (both in and out of the district) have found out about this program via visitations, PTA presentations, and films and slides which district people and I have made about the room. Last year, our local newspaper sent out a reporter who stayed most of the day and wrote an outstanding article. We were pleased that he gave a true report of the program. I believe it is a direct result of our room that at least five other rooms have now been started in our city.

SUMMING UP

Before becoming the teacher in the Resource Room, I always had, I feel, quite an exciting and stimulating classroom. There were lots of projects, and I feel that the children for the most part were interested and happy. However, I was definitely the one who structured the program. I was in charge and I seldom asked for the opinions of the children. I poured "information" or "facts" into them. I was usually convinced that the "quiet, orderly, hard workers" were the most capable and best students. It didn't enter my brain that the aggressive child might be bright but bored. I placed a great deal of emphasis on having an orderly classroom which reflected extreme neatness.

Working with the Resource Room has really opened my eyes. Every day is a learning experience for me. It's so amazing to watch children operate when no one is directing them. I'm astounded at art work produced by students I would least expect to have this talent. On the other hand, some of the nice, sweet, always-minding children can't do anything on their own.

One wonderful aspect of working in the Resource Room is that I am freed from providing rigid directions for students. For example, I never use dittoed sheets of directions with the children. I feel that the use of such dittoed materials is one of the biggest deterrents to creativity that a teacher can introduce into a classroom. A child's first experience in school is so free. But when they get to first and second grade and receive a good diet of dittoes they really tighten up.

Another of the beauties of the Resource Room program is that we have time to love one another, to learn how to get along with each other, to share, and to care for materials and supplies—in general, to have a great opportunity for character building to take place. I have many, many opportunities to talk to the children and to be friends with them.

If and when I return to a regular classroom, I would like to base it on interest centers. I would like the children to help in the development of centers which they feel to be important. I would like to do away with desks, have stations for belongings, and have the children make a plan for the day, moving from one center to the next according to their plan. If it proves impossible to operate a whole classroom as a Resource Room, I would still have at least part of the classroom organized in this way and would teach certain subjects by using this discovery method.

APPENDIX A: THE RESOURCE ROOM

Goals for the Resource Room are:

1   To supplement and enrich classroom learning experiences.
2   To provide many opportunities for individual work.
3   To give opportunities for children to develop creative abilities.
4   To stimulate self-direction in students.
5   To encourage decision making.
6   To provide an opportunity for self-responsibility as it relates to peers and materials.

The Resource Room at Jefferson has a variety of centers or areas. The centers change or are rearranged about every two weeks. A few centers do not change.

There are over 900 children in Jefferson School. Most of them come to the Resource Room about once every two weeks, sometimes more often if the teacher utilizes all her scheduled times. The teachers decide who will come and when they will come, within the schedule.

Hopefully, no child is deprived of coming because of unfinished work, etc. Hopefully, each child is sent to the room as a basic part of his classroom program. *All* children are welcome, regardless of learning ability or maturity level.

Centers or areas:

science projects, exploration	measurement (rice, water, etc.)
cooking	games
a store	puzzles
dress-up items	arts and crafts
books	listening–viewing
sand	blocks
live animals	easels
toy animals, soldiers, dinosaurs, etc.	playhouse (cardboard)
	telephones
models	music
rest area (couch, rockers)	feel, pinch, squeeze center
construction	weaving
clay	others

APPENDIX B: LETTER TO PARENTS

Dear Parents and Friends of the Jefferson School:

As many of you know, we have a Resource Room or Learning Center here at Jefferson. This room is open to all children in the school. The homeroom teachers and students make arrangements together for students' use of this facility. Mrs. Reetzke is the teacher assigned to this room.

At the present time, there are no funds available for the supplies and materials used in the Resource Room. Many materials are needed and will be put to use. If you have and could donate any of the following materials, we would appreciate having such items. We assume that these things are to be given and so could not be returned. There are some things that we could borrow, and we would make special arrangements.

Wilhold glue—gallon or full small bottles	plaster of paris
masking tape	knitting needles, crochet needles
Scotch tape	balls of usable yarn
models—new—inexpensive— 29–39 cents	shiny egg carriers (plastic foam)
clean baby food jars and lids	pipe cleaners or covered florist wire

2"- or 3"-plastic or clay flower pots (clean)

bags of dry beans, peas, rice, popcorn (for bean mosaics)

glass (strips—12" by 2" for making kaleidoscopes)

broken pieces of colored glass

drafting board (could be borrowed)

clean burlap

tools (hammer, screwdriver, pliers, wire cutters, drill, clamps, etc.)

balsa wood

felt—squares, etc.

goggles—smoked for glass blowing

asbestos gloves

propane torch—small

trays—metal or cardboard

slide projector—carousel, if possible—easy for children to use

slides you don't want—trips to national parks, etc.

papier-mâché

finger paints

flour—10 pounds

salt—10 pounds

plasticene modeling clay

food coloring

25 pounds of rabbit pellets

10 pounds of chicken mash

10 pounds of hamster mix

tropical fish

rock tumbler

dry cells, new

microscopes (not the type most children are given as gifts)

potter's wheel

loom

Barbie dolls and clothes

seeds

timers or hourglasses

woodburning set

747 model—new

Apollo models—new

model glue

model paint

typewriter—good condition

Childcraft

up-to-date World Book

rolls of insulated wire to use with dry cells, etc.

cages—animal

terrariums

cameras—cheap

developing tanks

developer and fixer solution

electric drill

new, inexpensive scrapbooks

hinges

stamps—if possible steamed off

electric skillet—good condition

used or old 16 mm. film

checkers

chess

radio—to be taken apart and put back together

clocks

Dri-Markers

watercolor felt pens

binoculars

telescope

hot plate—good

motors, engines that work

spray shellac

spray paint

splicer

slot car and/or Hot Wheels set

Visible Man or Woman

Please remember our offering box. It helps! Thank you.

APPENDIX C: SURVEY FORM

Would you consider the following items? Have a class discussion if possible.

> Be honest. Use back of sheet. How do you really feel about R.R.?

How do *you* feel the R.R. could be changed or improved? What types of things, displays, materials, etc., would you like it to include?

Teacher
_____
_____
_____
_____

What changes, improvements, additions do the boys and girls desire?

Students
_____
_____
_____
_____

Would you prefer sign-up or structured activities in the A.M. and open for free time in the P.M.? Or should we continue as now?

_____
_____

What displays or special activities would help your class? _____

_____
_____

What science or social studies units will you cover before school is over?

_____
_____

Your Name _____ (Further comments on back.)

CHAPTER 6

CLASSROOM INTEREST CENTERS

Betty J. Christianson and Darlene Fear

This chapter introduces the reader to a way of individualizing instruction through the organization of interest centers. The authors explain how one can organize the class, schedule the activities, and keep track of what is happening. This organization is explained for both lower and upper primary grades with accompanying charts and graphs. The tension between the "musts" and free choice activities is candidly discussed with the reader.

Before we can accept and value independent activities for children we must examine how children learn. In fact, we can ask ourselves as adults, how do we really learn? How did we learn to drive on the freeway? Was it really in Drivers' Education? Or was it when we got a license and a job or needed to travel the freeway to get to college? How did you ladies learn to sew a dress? Was it really in Home Economics, or did you learn it independently when you needed a dress quickly for a special occasion and hadn't the money to buy one? It didn't take you a semester as it might have in Home Ec. Yet perhaps it was only a short time after you had passed (or maybe failed) Home Ec that you had accomplished the sewing so rapidly. We could cite many, many examples of how rapidly we learned things that we *most wanted* and *most needed* to learn. John Holt, in his book *How Children Learn,* states:

> ... curiosity is hardly ever idle. What we want to know, we want to know for a reason. The reason is that there is a hole, a gap, an empty space in our understanding of things, or mental model of the world. . . . When the gap in our understanding is filled, we feel pleasure, satisfaction, relief. Things make sense again—or at any rate, they make more sense than they did.
>
> When we learn this way, for these reasons, we learn both rapidly and permanently. . . . The new piece of knowledge fits into the gap ready

for it, like a missing piece in a jigsaw puzzle. Once in place, it is held in, it can't fall out. We don't forget the things that make the world a more reasonable or interesting place for us, that make our mental model more complete and accurate.[1]

So it is with children. They learn best and most rapidly when they feel a need to fill an empty space in their understanding about something that is of interest to them. Tom feels no obligation to listen to his teacher tell the class about the dairy because he was raised on a dairy farm. He is more interested in finding out about snakes because he caught one yesterday. Of course, the teacher does not know this.

Nor is it possible to find out what gaps a child may have in his mental model. We can diagnose, question, and probe, but we cannot determine his understanding because, as Holt points out, (1) a child is unaware of much of his own understanding; (2) he hasn't the skill to put his understanding into words that he is sure we would understand; and (3) we don't have time to listen.

So what is our alternative in helping children fill gaps in their knowledge of the world? First, we need to believe that man is by nature a learning animal and that children have a natural style of learning, a style that fits their condition, their ways. We need to allow children to work more independently, seek their own levels of understanding, and use and improve the style of thinking and learning which is natural to them. Holt calls it a faith. He says we must bring as much of the world as we can into the school and classroom, give children as much help and guidance as they need and ask for, listen respectfully when they feel like talking, and then get out of the way. We can trust them to do the rest.

This chapter offers two approaches to individualization through the use of interest centers, one adaptable to lower grades and one for upper grades. The ideas for individualizing presented here revolve around *organization,* with the teacher functioning as the key in organizing and allowing opportunities for children to reach their potential through creative experiences. As you read this article please keep in mind that we are not attempting to provide a detailed account of how you should teach. The secret of an individualized program is that it allows for individual teacher and student creativity. The possibilities for growth are endless!

1. John Holt, *How Children Learn,* Pitman Publishing Company, New York, 1967, pp. 187–88.

Before implementing any new program, it is necessary to ask oneself, "Why do I want to change my program?" Initially you may consider broad, general goals for your children as a class, such as: (1) children will become self-directed; (2) children will be responsible for independent work; (3) children will become involved in what they do, when they do it, and how they do it. Later your goals will become more specific as individual needs become apparent. After diagnosing Gene's needs, you may want to state goals that apply specifically to him: (1) Gene will develop a more positive attitude toward reading; (2) Gene will develop a more positive self-image.

As your relationship with Gene grows, he will become an active part of the goal-setting process, thus sharing the responsibility. You may ask him, "What are some things you want to do better?" Goals such as the following may then result:

1   "I want to learn to write my own stories."
2   "I want to be a better tetherball player."

THE LOWER PRIMARY GRADES

Preplanning before the start of the school year is vital when implementing a new program. A method of organization which we have found to be effective is the Rotation System. The classroom is divided into four basic interest areas: Writing, Listening, Activities, and the Teacher-Center Area (see Figure 6.1).

The children are placed in four heterogeneous groups of eight children each. Heterogeneous grouping is suggested, rather than the usual homogeneous grouping, because it creates a climate in which children may more easily learn from one another. Close examination of cumulative folders is helpful in organizing balanced groups, with high and low achievers and leaders in each.

At the beginning of the day, each of the four groups is stationed at a different area in the room. They spend approximately thirty minutes at an area, then rotate as a group to the next area. Though the children are grouped, there is, nevertheless, a great deal of individualization taking place. For example, in the Teacher-Center Area, the teacher will initially meet with a group of approximately eight children. She may send two children from this group to the bookshelves to browse through books, while two other children from the same group quiz each other on vocabulary words through the use of flashcards.

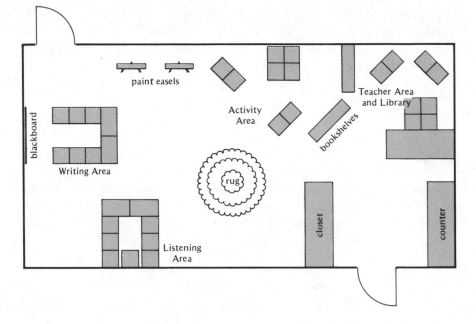

FIGURE 6.1   A CLASSROOM DESIGN

This leaves her with the four remaining members of the group who have been diagnosed as having a common skill deficiency, such as the inability to comprehend what they have read. On the following day, the four children who had the skill lesson may have a follow-up sheet pertaining to comprehension while the teacher meets with the remaining four to hear them read from their books, individually or in pairs.

A simple method for keeping track of the groups is through the use of the standard rotation chart (Figure 6.2). The chart designates each group by color and indicates the area in which each group is working at any given time. (On the first day, children should be provided with color-coded name tags to indicate the group to which they belong.)

Your classroom has basically been divided into four areas and from there you can create choices within each area and control the choices within a basic framework.

Writing Area   This area is composed of tables or a series of desks arranged in a ∪ shape facing a blackboard. There should be paper and pencils available at this area. For first-level children, a sample assignment could be anything from spelling on Mondays and Fridays to the copying of stories for handwriting practice.

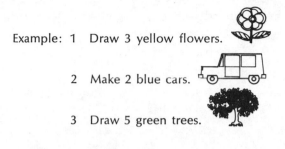

Example: 1 Draw 3 yellow flowers.

2 Make 2 blue cars.

3 Draw 5 green trees.

As the first-level child gradually learns to read, you eliminate the hints, such as three written as "3," "yellow" written with yellow chalk, and the pictures. The child ends up able to read all the instructions.

Always write the assignment on the blackboard, and provide two or three alternative tasks for the child to do when he finishes the assignment.

Example: 1 Copy the story.
2 Draw a picture or fun ditto.
3 Finish any work.

Listening Area or A.V. Area This area could contain a tape recorder, record player, or filmstrip projector with earphones. It is set up with a pre-taped lesson, timed for fifteen to twenty minutes, depending

Yellow	Blue	Red	Green
person	headphones	dice	pencil
pencil	person	headphones	dice
dice	pencil	person	headphones
headphones	dice	pencil	person

FIGURE 6.2 STANDARD ROTATION CHART

on the interest level of the child. If you have made a story tape following a book, provide a follow-up pertaining to the story.

Example: 1 Draw the 4 main parts of the story in sequence on paper folded in 4 boxes.

2 Draw your favorite part of the story.

3 Draw the main characters of the story.

4 Answer these 3 questions (if they do not read, tell them the questions aloud; they may answer "yes" or "no").

Activities and Games Area   On the first day of school you may want to set out a few self-explanatory games or puzzles for children. A choice chart could be hung in the activity area designating the choices available. This will be added to later as choices are increased.

Example: *Choice Chart*

1 Work a puzzle.

2 Use flashcards.

3 Draw a picture.

4 Use the blackboard (for practicing ABCs, writing any words he wishes, playing tic-tac-toe with a friend, etc.).

Teacher-Center Area   This area could consist of a bookcase library with pillows and a small table where you can meet with the children. Some of the children will be reading and looking at books while you are working with the others (diagnosing, listening to them read, holding conferences, and teaching directed lessons).

Getting Started

As the children enter the first day, each child will hunt for his desk, which he can identify by the colored name tag that you have made. Call the children together as a group and welcome them; then take them on a tour of the room and explain each of the four centers and what they will do when it is their turn to visit that center. The directions are given in advance to avoid interruptions from children asking, "What do we do now?" This is also the reason for alternative choices at each area; when a child finishes one activity he has something else to do until you are finished with your group.

Once you have explained the organization of the room to the children and have shown them the different types of learning opportunities available, you are ready to launch them into activities. Refer to your chart and ask who is wearing a blue name tag. "All the people with a blue name tag go to the Listening Area." Get the Blue Group seated, turn on the tape recorder, and make sure there are no problems. Then proceed to do the same with the remaining areas, ending with your Teacher-Center Area. This may take a little time, but it is time well spent, for it eliminates interruptions when you are involved at the Teacher-Center Area.

Have the Teacher-Center group go with you and read books until each child is called to visit with you; you can individually give your diagnostic tests to them while the others are reading.

At the end of about twenty minutes, ring a bell. Have children stop, clean up, and repeat with Level Two. The completion of the chart will take up your whole morning.

Example of a Daily Schedule
(Morning only)

8:30– 8:45	Opening exercises (roll, flag, sharing, milk money)
8:45– 9:00	Planning (a child reads the rotation chart aloud so that children know which area they go to first)
9:00– 9:30	1st Rotation
9:30–10:00	2nd Rotation
10:00–10:15	Recess
10:15–10:45	3rd Rotation
10:45–11:15	4th Rotation
11:15–11:30	Clean-up and evaluation of morning activities
11:30–12:30	Lunch

The morning program is devoted largely to language arts, although the creative arts are included as an independent activity in the Activity Area. The bulk of the mathematics program is covered during the afternoon. Children are divided into four homogeneous math groups. The teacher meets with two groups for a half hour each afternoon while the remaining groups are doing independent math work at their seats. Science, social studies, and physical education are usually integrated into the day as total class activities with independent research projects.

The whole procedure of orienting the children to the classroom environment and launching them into learning activities might take several days. There are young children who may never have been exposed to this type of learning situation. Be patient! As each day progresses, children will become accustomed to this daily routine. They will come to know it well and will be able to predict where they will be going next without looking at the chart. This is good. They are becoming independent. But be careful! They will also become bored if you do not grow with them, expanding the choices within each interest area. They will tire easily of listening and writing if you don't constantly challenge them.

In the first weeks your interest centers are still relatively large, equipped to handle groups of at least eight children at a time. As the children become more independent, you may want to create small centers within the large centers. For example, at the Listening Center, instead of having eight children doing the same tape-recorded lesson, you could set up the tape with four headsets and a lesson, and set up a story record and a filmstrip with a readable film for four children. Children then would be able to choose between these alternatives for that day.

Broadening of interests is also possible in the other areas. The Writing Center might offer boardwork, practice with letters using acetate folders, dittoed writing activities, creative stories, typing, and bookmaking. The child should be free to choose within this area the activities which interest him most.

Probably the most flexible of these areas can be the Activity Center. The teacher can incorporate a variety of activities such as painting, research, math games, social studies tasks, and all sorts of miscellaneous items.

The directed lesson in the Teacher Center may start out as a total group activity with all eight children, to be restructured when individual differences among the children become more apparent. For example, the teacher may meet with the Red Group as a total group and deal out verbal assignments such as, "Today I would like to read privately with Jeff, Mark, and Mary. The rest of you may choose one of these activities to do: read with a friend, read in the library, make a play, or practice your vocabulary words."

Keeping Track of Students' Work

Record keeping must be a cooperative venture in an individualized program. You might issue each student a folder in which to keep his work. Folders can be made of construction paper with an attached plan sheet on the cover (see Example A, page 111). The child will place his work inside the folder as he completes it at the different centers throughout the day. A sheet of graph paper may be attached to the inside of the folder for the child's independent record keeping of his math progress. If the child is on an independent math contract, this system of record keeping is excellent.

The children's folders are collected and checked each day by the teacher, and work is placed in a finished-work box to be put into the child's individual mailbox by a helper. Children check mailboxes before going home each day.

Anecdotal records are extremely important, especially in the area of reading. During conference time with parents they are very helpful in reviewing the child's progress.

You may also wish to keep a file box for reading with separate cards for each child. When you confer with a child you will want to write down book and pages read, problem words, and future needs, as well as the date of the conference.

Problems That May Occur

There are a few problems that may develop in the course of your program. Some children need more direction than others. You may wish to talk with the more dependent child and explain to him that you are going to help him plan his day until he is able to follow through on his assignments on his own. You will need to keep close tabs on him and observe his progress, rewarding growth with more responsibility for his own planning.

A problem pertaining to the rotation system is that there will be children who will not finish their work before the bell rings. It is important that you allow at least fifteen minutes extra time (perhaps before lunch) for all children to spend finishing their work. Children also need a few minutes at the end of each day to share work that they have completed, such as a creative story or a painting.

THE UPPER PRIMARY GRADES

Pre-planning and preparation is basically the same for upper primary grades as for the lower primary. When initiating new programs, the teacher must take responsibility to organize the room physically to coincide with the basic rotation chart of four teams and the variety of activity centers planned. The floor plan in Figure 6.3 is a sample.

After a few weeks of using this room, organizing, and establishing a routine, soliciting ideas from the children will surely result in a more creative plan.

In addition to the initial responsibility of arranging the room, the teacher must be resourceful in collecting a variety of materials to be used at the different centers. These could include games, manipulative aids, magazines, plants, animals, science collections, art supplies (cloth, paint, wood scraps obtained from lumber yards, crayons, odd objects for collages), and kitchen supplies such as vinegar, sugar, and salt for "kitchen chemistry." All of these materials are meant to set the stage for a rich environment with a world of things to do.

Getting Started

Initiating a program for upper primary children will be basically the same as for lower grades. One difference is that the children should be capable of accepting more responsibility for independent work due to

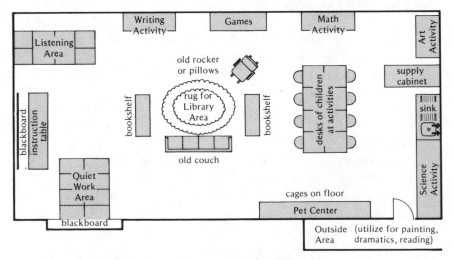

FIGURE 6.3   CLASSROOM DESIGN, UPPER PRIMARY

their acquired basic skills. However, consideration must still be given to children who lack experience and maturity in making decisions and accepting responsibility for independent work assignments. More time might also be allowed for children to plan and discuss solutions to problems that arise within the program.

The Rotation Chart shown in Figure 6.4 provides a more complex example of the basic four-group rotation plan discussed above. This variation is more suitable for the upper primary grades.

The chart assumes thirty-two children in the room with eight in each group. As shown, it is set up for reading. Team I begins the reading period by reading with the teacher. Team II is doing "quiet work," such as spelling, reading follow-up, penmanship, and so forth. Team III is listening to a tape or using other audio-visual equipment, such as a filmstrip projector or record player with story record. Team IV is involved in activities listed on the left side of the chart. The members of Team IV may all be working together, independently, or in small groups. As there are eight activities provided for the eight children making up the team, each child could engage in a different activity for eight days. On the left side of the chart, the activities are listed on tabs which may be inserted into or removed from the slits on the chart as the nature of activities is changed.

Any attention-getting signal, such as tapping tone bells, may be used to alert the children that it is time to stop working, tidy up the center or area in which they have been engaged, and move to the next activity. It is always worthwhile to take time to incorporate good habits of listening for instructions, taking care of materials, and keeping the centers organized and ready for others to use.

Maintaining the Program

When and how often would you use this plan? It can be used very effectively daily in twenty- or thirty-minute blocks of time, depending on the readiness of your children to work at tasks independently.

If you incorporate spelling, language, science, math, and other areas of the curriculum at your different centers, you can feel very justified in spending the entire morning involved with this rotation program. Your afternoon could then be devoted to Social Studies committee work and other group activities such as physical education and music.

Now the big question, "How often must centers be changed?"

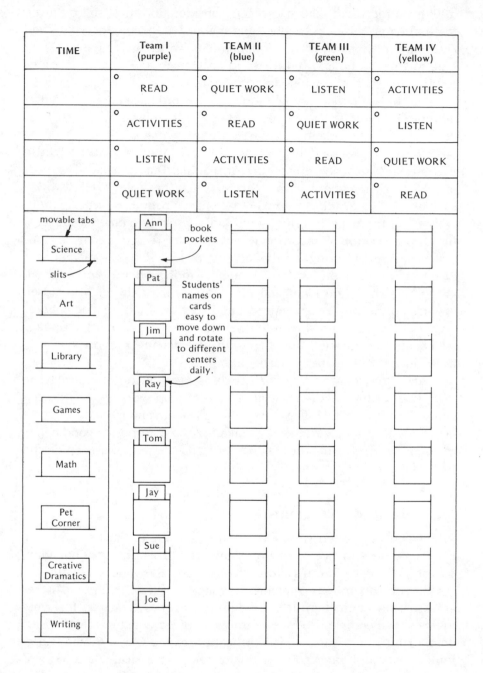

TIME	Team I (purple)	TEAM II (blue)	TEAM III (green)	TEAM IV (yellow)
	READ	QUIET WORK	LISTEN	ACTIVITIES
	ACTIVITIES	READ	QUIET WORK	LISTEN
	LISTEN	ACTIVITIES	READ	QUIET WORK
	QUIET WORK	LISTEN	ACTIVITIES	READ

movable tabs

Science

slits

Art

Library

Games

Math

Pet Corner

Creative Dramatics

Writing

Ann — book pockets

Pat

Jim

Students' names on cards easy to move down and rotate to different centers daily.

Ray

Tom

Jay

Sue

Joe

FIGURE 6.4   ROTATION CHART, UPPER PRIMARY

Reading, quiet work, and listening would have to be changed daily, because you would be presenting a child with new tasks in these areas. Of course these three areas would not be hard to change because your instruction naturally would differ daily.

The Quiet Work Area could include a variety of written activities such as spelling, writing words in sentences, using them in a story, or completing pages in the workbook. Other assignments could be an English lesson, such as writing business or personal letters; a dictionary assignment, such as finding five new words and writing meanings or finding the names of five animals and drawing a picture of them; or asking children to finish a story which you have begun on the blackboard. There are endless ways to provide a quiet, interesting, and challenging writing lesson without a ditto.

The fourth category on the top of the chart refers to activities listed along the side of the chart. As the chart is organized (eight activities and eight children) it could remain the same for eight days. Thus you would need to change activities in a week and a half. This may appear to be a big task, but upon closer examination you can see it will not be too time consuming or difficult. For example, *Science* could be simple "kitchen science," using items from the kitchen for testing materials that dissolve or that have fat or acid. A microscope or magnifying glass could be provided, with children selecting items to examine such as hair, a leaf, etc. Or a box of shells or stones to classify and name could be supplied. *Art* could be any simple project, using a variety of available materials—scraps of fabric, beans, seeds for a collage, magazines, paints, a variety of media. *Library* would simply be an area where children could use reference books and library books to read and plan projects such as dioramas and book reports. *Games* could be different games you as a teacher have accumulated or those that children make up or bring in to share (chess, dominoes, etc.). *Math* could be measuring activities, graphing assignments ("How many children in the room have blue clothes, red clothes, brown eyes?" etc.), ordinary flashcards, jars of beans for estimating, rules for measuring, geoboards and other manipulative thinking math activities.

The *Pet* Center could include cages of rats, snakes, fish, etc., for children to observe, read about, write stories about, handle, feed, and care for. How fascinating for children to build mazes to test the rats' ability to travel! How about timing the rate and recording the progress and growth of baby animals? The *Creative Dramatics* Center could have puppets (commercial puppets could be provided, or children could make simple finger puppets out of paper or ice cream sticks) to be used in acting out stories or plays the children had written or read about. Old clothes (especially hats) could be used for dress-up or planning plays. The *Writing* Center could be an area where children learn to write haiku, cinquain, or free verse, or perhaps start writing a book of their own.

There are literally hundreds of activities that could be used as interest centers. One just needs to let the imagination wander to discover new and challenging ideas for children to discover and explore. But keep in mind the fact that as both you and the children grow and broaden your experience in individualizing, you may find the need for totally re-vamping the centers. You have grown with the children and both of you are now able to accept more independence within the standards you have already established.

Monitoring

There are some basic musts or assignments that you are going to want all your children to accomplish by the end of the day, for example, writing, completing two pages of math, reading at least one story. Write these on your blackboard under "Musts." There are also individual seat-work activities you may want certain children to work on. These can be inserted in that child's weekly folder. On the outside of the folder is a calendarlike plan sheet for the week. On this the child records his planned activities for each day as it arrives (Example A). The teacher has a master plan schedule with the list of her lessons for the day posted within sight of all (Example B).

The children plan the day's activities with the teacher and discuss their plans. They then check the master schedule to see when they are to meet with the teacher, filling this in on their plan sheet. Next they check their assigned "Musts" and fill those in. They may do these tasks at any time they choose, as long as it doesn't interfere with their meetings with the teacher. The rest of the time is theirs to explore the various interest areas set up in the room. It is important at first that they write down and follow through with the choices which they have made. They are becoming accustomed to a new way of independent working.

Problems will arise such as, "What shall we do when fifteen children all plan art first?" or, "What about the child who doesn't follow

Example A

NAME				
Mon.	Tues.	Wed.	Thurs.	Fri.
Read				
Art				
Games				
Write				
SRA				
Miss Fear				

Example B

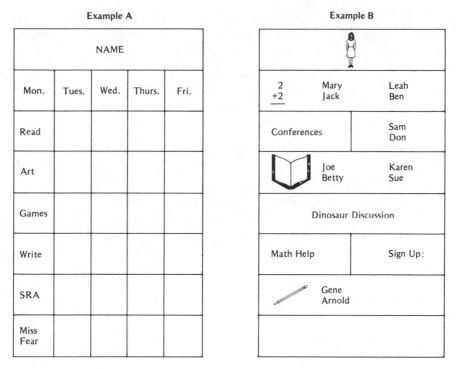

2 +2	Mary Jack	Leah Ben
Conferences		Sam Don
	Joe Betty	Karen Sue
Dinosaur Discussion		
Math Help		Sign Up:
	Gene Arnold	

his plan?" Here's where flexibility comes in. Discuss with the children how many people should be at the different areas at one time. Explain that if the area is full, they should plan another activity and go back later. If a child doesn't follow through on his plan, he may need to discuss with you why one should plan: "The plan is like mother's grocery list; it helps us remember all we have to do today." You may need to assist him with planning until he is able to plan independently.

You'll find that with this system you are much more free to work with small groups and zero in on remedial work. You can start from a very structured situation, meeting with four reading groups (on alternate days) in the afternoon, and move into a very flexible organization, meeting with children with specific needs and interests. The conference is an integral part of teaching in this manner. It is necessary to have a private time when a child can read for you and meet with you, even if it is just to share a vital experience important to him. Try to set aside at least a half an hour each day for conferences and let the children sign up for them.

We have taken you through the steps of classroom organization from a limited choice situation leading into an endless variety of classroom experiences for children. The children will take the steps with you and will grow capable of much more self-direction than when they started. The ultimate goal in using interest or activity centers is to involve each child in creating and utilizing his own environment. Truly, this is an individualized program.

CHAPTER 7

FIVE YEARS OF INDIVIDUALIZATION

Jane O'Loughlin

This teacher recounts a variety of teaming experiences which led to the emergence of her own partnership with another teacher. The chapter describes the daily activities of second and third graders in an individualized program. Special emphasis is given to spelling, with explicit directions for initiating and maintaining an individualized spelling program, and for tape recording tests. The author imparts a sense of the renewed dedication of two experienced teachers who replaced "the deadly routine" with "the joy of teaching and learning."

This year I am a member of a team dedicated to the belief that each child is a unique individual with his own special needs and desires as well as his own rate and style of learning. While each child is constantly developing, growing, changing, and learning, he must encounter experiences which will build his self-image and enhance his relationships with other human beings.

There is nothing new in the above statement. It might almost suffice as a general description of the duties of a teacher: to take each child where he is and lead him further along the way. But, as anyone who has ever attempted to reach each and every one of thirty squirming youngsters knows, it is not an easy task. Rather, it is a teacher's Utopia! A few reach it, most struggle toward it, and some are overwhelmed by it. Have I found the road to Utopia? No! There is no one road. But, together with another person, I have found and started along a path which has led both of us to a glimpse of it.

We are excited about our path! It is flexible, ever changing, and always demanding. You probably will not follow our path all of the way because you are as unique as your children. You might go along with us for a while and then take another road that is better for you.

You might begin on your own and meet us along the way. Or, hearing about our journey, you may decide it is not for you.

HOW IT ALL BEGAN

Looking back before the start of our adventure, I see two people with a love of children and a combined total of twenty-four years of teaching experience. Each of us had her own classroom, but both had child-centered as opposed to autocratic classrooms. There were opportunities for free time with games, puzzles, paint, and clay always available. Children were free to move quietly about the room when the teacher was not talking. But, we realize now, the teacher was talking most of the time.

Each of us had three or four reading groups. While children sometimes moved from group to group, the majority stayed in the same reading group from September to June. All children had the same new spelling words on Monday, and all took a test on Friday. All children had the same social studies and science lessons. Math was the only area in which some individualization had taken place. Generally there were two groups, sometimes three, with one group being given their math books sooner than the others. This group was allowed to work to a certain page and then stop. Lessons were given and then they proceeded to a stipulated point. The other group worked page by page with the teacher. As teachers, each of us went her own way with her own class. However, our personal relationship was such that ideas and materials were shared and problems were discussed.

How did the metamorphosis take place? It began five years ago when our school became one of the eighteen schools involved in the League of Cooperating Schools. These League schools felt the need for changes in education but were not committed to any particular change. Each school was to attempt the kinds of changes which would most benefit its own children. Our staff spent a year listening to experts who gave us no answers. How wise they were! They made us find our own way. By June, we had a school goal: the self-directed child. We all agreed that only a child who was self-directed could survive in our rapidly changing world. Each teacher decided for herself the course she would take in order to reach this goal.

The second year was the year of the four-man team. Teaming was new to all of us, and we were most eager to try it. We had four teachers and 120 second grade boys and girls in an egg-crate type of school.

We ability-grouped in the academic areas and then spent all year trying to find a way to overcome this type of grouping. Unfortunately, we did not succeed. We made great strides in allowing children to make choices, to plan their time, and to work independently in many ways. However, the choices were confined to social studies, science, and art.

The next September some walls came down and sliding doors were installed. It was the year of the five-man team with second and third graders. Due to a fire wall, we had a two-room and a three-room situation. We were constantly striving to find ways to group children other than by ability. We spent endless hours arranging and rearranging children, teachers, and programs. It seemed we could only do the things we wanted to do with more teachers and more room. We found numbers unwieldy and communication difficult. The five-man team did not survive the year. It broke into a team of three and a team of two. The team of two continued but the team of three, with less compatible personalities, gradually reverted into three self-contained classrooms.

We had learned a lot! For us, the surviving team, communication was easy. Our two-room set-up helped, and our philosophy concerning children was similar, as was our method of relating to children. We worked well together; each was willing to do more than her share. Our first step was to explain the situation to the children. We told them that the original team was too big and we would now be a team of Rooms 6 and 7. These boys and girls had been working in the mornings with five different teachers in classroom situations which were relatively homogeneous and isolated from each other. We were now one large heterogeneous group with two teachers.

· THE TWO OF US

Now that we were working together, the two of us began in earnest to individualize. The following sections explain how we developed individualized programs in math, reading, social studies, and spelling. Throughout, I have tried to provide suggestions for teachers who would like to begin similar programs.

The Math Program

Since we both like having children work independently in math, we decided to return to that technique, eliminating math groups except when needed. We spent two days determining where the children were and what their immediate needs might be. A quick show of hands told us that approximately half of the children were working prior to page 125 in the math book and about half were working beyond this point. The first day all who were working in the first 125 pages took their books to one side of the room. The others went to the opposite side without math books to work on math games with a teacher. The doors were closed. A list was made of the children in the group and the page number they were working on was recorded. Notes were taken in regard to any specific problems the children felt they had. Each child then looked over his next math page. Those who needed help brought their books to the front of the room. A quick glance showed several were ready for a new concept that would require a lesson. These children were given a review worksheet to do for that day and their names were recorded for a lesson in the near future. The remaining children were helped with their pages. The second day we followed the same procedure, reversing the youngsters.

We made simple record sheets with children's names along the side, page numbers across the top, and red lines indicating which pages introduced a new concept. All children who were at a red line or almost there were grouped for that lesson or lessons and then proceeded on their own. One teacher would teach a group lesson while the other was available to help the children working independently. All math pages were corrected and recorded by the teachers. All errors were corrected at the beginning of the next math period before new work could be started.

Reading

In contrast to math, our reading program was a shambles! Neither of us had ever taught reading except in groups. Some of these children had been with us in our groups but many had been with the other three teachers. Once again we made a list: name of child, name of book, and place in book. While all were using the same state series, there was a wide spread, and to place everyone in a nice, neat reading group was an impossibility. We had to let some children leave the reading group situation. We grouped the slower youngsters and those who were unfortunate enough to be on a particular story, or very close to it, in a particular book. The others were allowed to go ahead on their own, one unit at a time. We spot-checked and worked with them when we were not with the groups. We checked with them at the end of each unit, and no one was allowed to start a new unit until one of us had introduced it.

It wasn't long before dissension appeared in the ranks. Children began asking if they had to read with a group; others asked if they could go ahead to the next story. Our groups eventually dissolved and children were proceeding through the books and the workbooks at their own rate. We kept track of their progress through the workbook pages, using a record sheet with the name of the book and a check for a completed or corrected page. File cards were used to note progress and problems.

It was a gradual process, for, while the children were eager to try their wings, we were reluctant to let them go. When a child was absent, he no longer had to try to catch up to his group or join some other group that had been reading behind him in the same book; instead, he started in where he had left off. Knowing the material as well as we did, we would call groups together anticipating a story for which background information or certain word attack skills would be needed. Sometimes we invited children to meet after a story was read to discuss the characters, their actions, and possible outcomes or ramifications. We listened to children read by ones, twos, or threes. We had "Reading Parties": children who had finished a certain unit formed a small circle, voted on their favorite story from that unit, and volunteered to read orally their favorite page. We liked our program. Sometimes we felt superfluous, and that hurt our egos, but the children loved reading independently.

ON OUR OWN

The following year, our fourth with the League, we were on our own—a team of two plus a shared aide for an hour and a half a day. Both of us liked having our children pace themselves in math so we decided to try the idea of pacing in reading. It had worked toward the end of the previous year, but would it work earlier in the year? Neither of us could live with the idea that second graders should read any book they chose. We felt library books from which they could choose were too limited for a year's program. We also felt a need for a sequential program of skills. This was the year the state of California switched from a standard reading series to multi-difficulty textbooks from many publishers. The books were assigned to schools on the basis of the number of disadvantaged, average, and advantaged children enrolled in a particular grade in a specific school. We were faced with a potpourri of six new reading series, with varying numbers of each.

We decided to begin school with the familiar texts. As workbooks were no longer supplied for these books, we went through our files and combined all the worksheets we already had for the books and made worksheets to fill in the missing spaces. The worksheets were placed in file folders, which were put into labeled vegetable bins. As the children finished their story, they found their worksheet, asked for help if it was needed, and then placed the completed work in a labeled box. All work was corrected and recorded. Any child who needed help was seen individually. As the children worked along in their first teacher-assigned book, we prepared similar files for the new books from the publisher's ditto masters. When the children finished their book they were allowed to choose their next book from any that were available. Through the year we gradually expanded our files and by the end of the year we had eight or nine books with the accompanying work.

OUR PROGRAM TODAY

Our present team consists of sixty-one children—forty-six second graders and fifteen third graders; two teachers; one volunteer mother who comes to us faithfully three days a week from 8:45 until 12:00; and one paid aide who works with us every day from 8:45 until 11:45. We have two rooms which function as one. The sliding doors are closed only for films and then only because one room does not have curtains (see Figure 7.1).

The children may sit anywhere they wish and with whom they please. They are free to move around the room, to work at a table or on the floor. They seek help from each other or from us. They choose many of their activities and the way in which they will learn.

The Reading Program

Because we were more familiar with our reading books, we were able to start our reading program more quickly this year. Our third graders chose their own book and began to read independently on the first day of school. Second graders were grouped according to their first grade reading records. We read with these groups for the first two

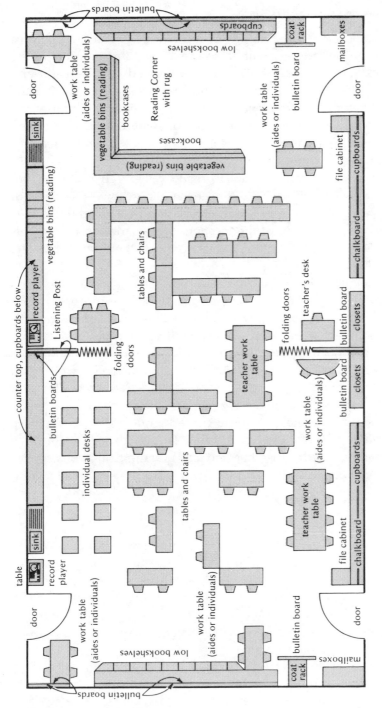

FIGURE 7.1   OUR ROOM PLAN

119

weeks of school, switching groups at the end of the first week. This way we had an opportunity both to hear each child read and to assess his strengths and weaknesses. Notations were made on file cards and compared at the end of the day. At the beginning of the third week the procedure for reading independently was explained, and those who wanted to go ahead were allowed to do so. Some did, many did not. Every day the opportunity is given for independent or group reading, until presently only three or four children are not working independently. These children do not want to read by themselves and do not want to be in a group. They are not necessarily our slowest readers but they need the security of a personal relationship with an adult. So they continue to read with one of the teachers or the aide for a large portion of the school year. We don't want to move them until they feel they are ready.

The plan of having each individual select his own textbook and proceed through it at his own rate constitutes a large portion of our reading program. However, our shelves are stacked with approximately 150 to 200 different storybooks. These are always available to the children and no worksheets or follow-up work is required. In addition to our classroom library there is a school library. Occasionally we suggest a Library Day, when everyone selects and reads library books, or a Poster Day, when everyone who wishes to do so chooses a library book, reads it, and makes a colorful poster about his book. We have multiple copies of some books so it is not unusual to see two or three children reading a story together and collaborating on a poster. We also have some copies of textbooks for which we have not made worksheets. These are called "fun books." Many of the children keep these books in their desks, reading them as the mood strikes, telling us about them informally, and finishing them or not as they please. Those books that are completed are so noted on the reading card for that child.

Our phonic and word attack skills are taught individually and to groups. The first semester each child had a fifteen- or twenty-minute group lesson. He also had individual lessons when they were needed. This was usually determined by the particular story he was reading or the worksheet he was doing. Now we have group lessons only when we feel there is a particular need.

We utilize the tape recorder and the Listening Post in our reading program. We have accumulated sets of six or eight paperback books and have taped the stories with one or more voices. We have also done this with some hardback books containing many stories. On

Monday, the story of the week is put on the board. Children choose to listen and read along as many times as they wish during that week. If we are using an anthology, we put the beginning and ending pages along with the names of the stories and poems. We try to limit listening time to five or ten minutes, simply because we have found this to be enough for most children. Children operate the tape recorder by themselves after the first few times. If, near the end of the week, interest has been exhausted, we either put on a new story or remove the activity. If a story is very popular or children have been too busy to listen, we hold it over until all are satisfied. We find children enjoy reading along with the tape and are often motivated to read the book by themselves or to choose a related book.

At the beginning of each reading period we announce the names of the children we want to see first on that day, usually from three to five each. We also assign one or two children to read with our adult aides. If older students are helping that day, we ask who would like to read with them and assign them two or three readers. Our student helpers work with one child at a time. With the first child, the helper goes over the new vocabulary and listens to an oral reading of the story. The child then gets his worksheet, and if he needs help with it the older student stays with him. In the meantime, the second child has finished reading his story to himself and is now ready to read orally to the helper. Helpers who arrive unexpectedly or after the reading period has begun are either assigned a child with whom to work or else they write their name on the chalkboard and children who wish to read with them sign up to do so. All helpers report briefly to us on the progress of their students.

Perhaps one of our most successful plans has been assigning pupils to read together. Sometimes the slower child will read to a faster one, receiving help and direction with his work. At other times we pair children of fairly equal ability; and then again we may have the more advanced reader read his story to the slower reader. Generally one day a week we have a work-together day. On this day, all children are assigned a partner. We prepare the list in advance and read it to the class. We pair children we feel will work well together, regardless of sex, age, or ability. We feel this device has aided in drawing our large group of sixty-one into a more cohesive unit. Children who might never become friendly are given the opportunity to meet, to work together, and to help one another.

Another way the children help us is by giving vocabulary tests.

Here we have one rule. The person giving the test must have read that particular book. Children love playing teacher, and the honor of giving and then correcting a vocabulary test is a much-sought-after one.

A word of warning: The noise level is high! And, since we once insisted on absolute quiet during the reading hour, this has been quite an adjustment for us. Now we often sit with a child on each side of us and one or two in front of us, each completely oblivious to the others, the different stories they are reading, or the help they may be receiving. Other children come to us for help and the readers continue. Occasionally their ears perk up and they will sit and listen as one child reads something particularly exciting and then back they go to their own story. We are constantly amazed at how children can block out extraneous noise, but then maybe they have been blocking us out for years without our knowing it.

The children proceed through a teacher-planned spelling program at their own rate. They give each other spelling tests at any time of the day and on any day of the week. When a child is ready for a test, he has a test. These tests are also on tape, so a child may choose to take his test this way.

All of the activities we have done in the past we continue to do today. Only now every day is a different day. The deadly routine is gone. Children still read to us singly or in small groups, only now it is because they ask to do so or we ask to listen to them. It is a mighty nice feeling to hear a small voice ask, "Can I read to you?" We still have our "Reading Parties" but they are voluntary and often child-suggested. Some days we assign certain children to read and work with each other. Some days they may read to a helper from another room. Some days a child may spend the whole time reading a fascinating library book. There is no pressure to stay with a group. There is no stigma attached to reading in a particular book, because maybe at this moment in time the best reader in the room is reading in the same book. We love it!

Social Studies

We wanted our children to have reading experiences in addition to those of the reading hour. We wanted them to read in order to find and to discuss common information. Forty-six second graders and fifteen third graders presented us with a wide range of reading abilities for instructional purposes. It was then we had a brilliant idea. The tape recorder! The children all enjoyed the stories on the Listening Post. Could we utilize this for the fifteen third graders? Could eight read along at the Listening Post while seven worked and then switch places, much as we used to do with our old reading groups? Could we play a tape loudly enough for the large group of second graders to hear and would they be able to follow along in the book? We knew the books were too difficult for many of our little ones to read by themselves. This way, they would at least be hearing the information and perhaps it would help their reading.

We decided to tape a few social studies lessons for each book. We taped an introduction for each lesson, much as we might talk to the children in a group. Then, as we read the text we called attention to pictures and explained unusual words. On the third grade tape an explanation was given as to how the follow-up work was to be done.

We decided to bring all the second graders to one side of the room, turn the tape recorder up full blast, give each child a marker and see if he could follow along. Five of these children were out of the room at this time in a special reading class. This left us with forty-one. We asked for three upper graders to come in and help the children learn to keep their places. The tape recorder was placed in the center of the room, and everything worked so beautifully we couldn't believe it! Then came the discussion time. They all wanted to talk at once. At least we knew they were interested. The planned discussion time was shortened and we broke into groups. Those who wished to continue a discussion went with the teacher. The others drew a picture or wrote a few sentences about what they had just read.

At the same time, we were following our original plan with the third graders. We had decided to allocate two periods for their first lesson, thereby allowing plenty of time for the lesson, the discussion, and the follow-up work. It was a wise decision. Everything went smoothly. We chose the eight boys to go to the Listening Post first while the seven girls had a free work time. While the girls listened to the recording, the teacher discussed the lesson with the boys and then started them on their follow-up work. Then she was ready for the girls' discussion group. The following day all worked independently, and the teacher wandered between these children and the larger group.

The next time the third grade was to listen to the tape, the girls asked if they could work by themselves without the tape. Most of them were very capable readers and they wanted to work in the library by themselves. Permission was granted and from that day on a lesson always began with the questions: "Who wants to work at the Listening Post?" "Who wants to work in the library?" Those who went to the library had new and unusual words or concepts quickly explained to them before they left the room. They met for their discussion when they returned. These children helped each other, and occasionally one would return for help, taking the information back to the others. It is interesting to note that only occasionally did a boy choose to work by himself. The boys were delighted at being able to listen to the tape and follow along in the book. They also realized they needed more help with the follow-up work, and by remaining in the classroom help was more readily available. However, the decision was theirs.

Now we had a changed situation. We were both available while the boys were at the Listening Post. We decided to hold our second grade discussion group first, utilizing both teachers. We took approximately twenty children each, in a random manner. The discussions centered upon the previous lesson and an introduction to the new lesson. This was also the time we would make group charts and stories, listen to someone read a report, plan some of our follow-up activities, and form our committees. After listening to the tape, it was individual work time—pictures, stories, worksheets, reports, dioramas, murals, related library books, plays, or whatever each child or group of children chose to do.

The third graders continued to enjoy their program. But when we were a little more than halfway through the second grade book, some of the second grade children asked to read and work by themselves and some wanted to read with the teacher. Others, however, still wanted to listen to the tape. So we have adopted this plan: We set the tape recorder in the library corner, and the teacher who is working with the third grade boys keeps an eye on this group. The other teacher reads with some of the children in a circle and supervises those working alone. Each child makes his own choice each time the book is used. The largest group is always gathered around the tape recorder.

The use of the tapes gives the children a common body of knowledge. Those who are not fluent readers are not struggling to keep up with the others, while the child who can read and absorb material quickly is not waiting for a slower child. A child who is absent or out of the room does not miss a lesson. When he returns, it is a simple matter to put the tape on in the Listening Post. While he misses the discussion, he still has the information that the others have been given and is better able to participate in related activities.

We feel that taping these lessons accomplished our purposes. The children are provided an additional reading experience, and they have shown us evidence of their increasing ability to make decisions and choices as well. We find the teacher on the tape is able to hold her audience completely and consistently. Children who are able to choose a learning style that suits them for a particular day are interested and attentive. The teacher, freed by the tape, is able to give help when and where it is needed.

We also find that we frequently are able to have total group activities which relate to both levels. For example, all the children wove folders after the second graders had a unit on clothing and the third graders had studied the people of the Andes Mountains who raised sheep, spun wool, and wove blankets. We all made bread. Those who had been studying about the use of corn and cornmeal made corn bread, while those who had read about a trip to a bakery made white bread.

Other Programs

We are also individualizing in various ways in our other programs. The children proceed through a teacher-planned math program at their own rate. The science program is similar to the social studies program. Some units are chosen by the teachers and some by the students. The children generally have a choice as to how they will study a unit. If using the state textbook, they may listen to the teacher on a tape and then read along with the teacher's taped lesson. They may prefer a teacher and class discussion combined with independent work in the text or related books. They may work independently in the Instructional Materials Center, using the resources there or taking classroom books with them.

HOW TO DO IT

If you would like to begin a program of this sort, perhaps you might let the children go off on their own gradually as we did the first year. If you wish to plunge in to the stage we are now, be prepared to feel unneeded at times; to feel frustrated when a child selects a book you know is too easy for him (generally he has just finished a difficult book and chances are good his next selection will be more challenging); to be exasperated when a child reads only one story and does only one worksheet (tomorrow he'll probably do three). But also be prepared for happy, busy children who are reading, reading, reading!

Getting Ready

Before the school year begins, you should allow plenty of time for preparation. Here is a minimal list of materials which should be ready in advance:

1   Textbooks of varying levels of difficulty, and as many as possible (keep adding more through the year).

2   Worksheets, either teacher-made or commercial, to go with each book.

3   Folders for worksheets. Each folder should be labeled with the name of the story for which the worksheet is prepared (for the benefit of the children) and the number of the worksheet, if it is commercially produced (for ease in recording).

4   A box or vegetable bin for each book. Label the box with the title of the book and place in it the proper folders, arranged according to the order in which the stories occur in the book.

5   Recording forms arranged by units or numbers and stapled together with the name of the book on the front.

A recording form (see Figure 7.2) can be used for all reading books with numbered worksheets. The teacher writes the name of the book on the first page, assembles as many sheets as she will need, and staples them together. The same form can be used as a check sheet to record other information—number of library books read, number of book reports completed, spelling test results, or pages completed in a math book.

An alternate recording form (Figure 7.3) can be assembled by units with abbreviations replacing numbers. A blank ditto is made (to conserve dittos) and the teacher writes in book, unit, and story. The same code is used.

First Day

Display the books. Show the children the worksheet boxes or the workbooks that go with each text. Explain that this year those who would like to read by themselves and work by themselves may do so. Make it clear that each person will choose his own book, get his own

Name											
Denise	☆	☆	☆	☆	− /	☆	[☆]	☆	☆		
Gary	☆	☆	☆	[☆]	☆	☆	☆	☆			
Mike	☆	−☆2	☐								
Sharon	[☆]	[☆]									

CODE: ☆ − correct .   ☐ − see teacher

−☆2 − 2 wrong, corrected   [☆] − corrected

FIGURE 7.2   RECORDING FORM 1

worksheet (show them where and how), and place it in the proper box for correcting after it is finished. Tell them that anyone who needs help with the story or the work is to come to you. Explain that after reading the first story, anyone who wishes to go on to the next story may do so, that they may read as many stories in one day as they wish as long as they read at least one; and that those who wish to read in a group may do so. Allow the children to look over the books and, if possible, to choose their books themselves. Some may be ready to begin working now. Be prepared for confusion.

Second Day

Repeat the explanation of the procedure. Help children who have not done so to select books. Provide an opportunity for children to change

The Little White House						Unit 1	
Name	At Home	Flip & S.	Flip W. to H.	Little Chairs	Sur. for F.	Funny Bunny	Vocab.
Paul	☆	☆					
Steve	☆	☆	☆	☆	☆		

FIGURE 7.3   RECORDING FORM 2

books if they think their book is too difficult for them. Expect to have to give a great deal of help with finding the proper worksheets and placing completed work in the proper boxes.

Third Day

Offer the opportunity of a reading group situation. You will still be busy helping children to find their worksheets, to follow directions, and to place their work in the proper box.

Remember, not all sixty-one of our children followed this procedure on the first day of school. Only our fifteen third graders were involved; and we allowed five or six of them into the reading corner at a time to choose their books. The second graders were using teacher-assigned books in reading groups. After the second week, they began to go ahead on their own, reading their stories and getting their own worksheets. They finished their books on different days. The only part of the procedure that was entirely new to them was the opportunity to choose their own reading book.

Keeping Track

During the first week of school try to have a get-acquainted conference with each child. On a file card record things like: brothers, sisters, pets, likes, dislikes, and book chosen. Have the child read to you so you can assess the appropriateness of the book for him, but make no oral judgments. If the book is too hard, he will find it out for himself. As you meet with the child throughout the year, continue to record the books he chooses and to note his progress. Make brief notations for future reference. Can he read fluently? Does he use expression? How does he attack a new word? Can he answer questions about what he has read? Try not to feel frustrated if at the end of the first week you have not reached every child for a conference. The first week is the hardest for you because the whole situation is so totally new to the children. Don't overwhelm them with too many choices the first day. As some children approach the end of their first textbook, quietly set out two or three other books and the accompanying work. The children will be looking and listening. When it is time to select the second book, many will have already decided which one they want.

Spelling It Out

In describing our experiences earlier in this chapter, I have gone into some detail concerning our handling of some of our programs, such as reading and social studies; and I hope the suggestions just presented above will help you to get started in similar programs of your own. However, I touched only lightly on the subject of spelling. The following suggestions may be useful for planning and setting up your own spelling program.

Getting Organized Our system for keeping track of pupil progress in spelling relies on the use of "spelling strips" and accompanying test cards.

To prepare the spelling strips you will need the following materials:

36" tagboard
Library pockets
Construction paper, 6" $\times$ 9"
Writing paper, 6" $\times$ 9"
One tongue depressor per child
File cards, 5" $\times$ 8"
A basic vocabulary list

Cut tagboard into strips, 4" wide and 36" long. Print six or seven words on each library pocket. Arrange pockets from the bottom to the top, six pockets per strip. Make sure to leave a space between pockets so when tongue depressors are inserted they will not hide the words for the next pocket. Label strips A, B, C, etc., and label pockets 1 through 6. Attach strips to a bulletin board which children can reach.

Using a black felt tip pen, print each child's name on a tongue depressor. Make a small test booklet for each child, using five or six sheets of writing paper with a construction paper front and back. Print the word "Spelling" and the child's name on the cover.

Make five or six identical test cards for each strip, using 5"$\times$8" file cards (Figure 7.4). Arrange the words

FIGURE 7.4   TEST CARD

A					
A¹	**A²**	**A³**	**A⁴**	**A⁵**	**A⁶**
a	red	and	one	where	play
go	little	to	run	at	we
me	come	my	look	can	for
in	yellow	blue	funny	you	up
big	I	see	it	make	down
the	am	is	two	help	jump
not	here				

according to letter strip and pocket number. When a test is requested, cards are ready for use. You can hand the card to a child and say, "Please give Test A3 to Jean."

Prepare a Teacher Record Card (Figure 7.5) for each strip, with pocket number across the top. As the individual's tongue depressor is placed in a pocket record his name on a corresponding Teacher Record Card along with any misspelled words. As a child moves up the pockets, move his name on the teacher's card, as shown. These cards need frequent replacement as different children are progressing each day.

A glance at the card tells you that Bill, Mary, Bob, and John are progressing nicely. Kay is having trouble with "yellow." She missed "yellow" when taking test A2. She missed it again when she took A3. She is still studying it along with A4. The teacher knows Jean has been absent so she will concentrate on Jenny today and see if she can help Kay.

Recording in this manner tells you which children are at which

FIGURE 7.5   TEACHER RECORD CARD

A					
1	2	3	4	5	6
	~~Bill~~	Jean	Kay	Bob	Jenny
	~~Mary~~	yellow	Mary	where	
	Bill	~~Mary~~	one	help	
	little	~~Bob~~	John		
	~~Kay~~	~~John~~			
	~~yellow~~				

level, as you will have similar cards for lists A through F. However, it does not tell you how long a child has been at a certain level.

An alternate method relies on the Dated Record Card (Figure 7.6), which is changed weekly. Boys and girls are listed on separate cards for speedier identification. Requests for tests are written in colored ink. This facilitates identification of children who are to take a test on a certain day and aids in pinpointing the length of time between individual tests. Since color is not practical here, I have used the letter "T" to denote a test. The + sign indicates previously misspelled words which the child has not yet mastered and eliminates the necessity of re-recording them.

It is very important that you keep your records current. We try to see that each child has at least one test a week. We find, once the program is progressing, that the children rarely miss more than one word in a test. They seem to know when they are truly ready to take a test. But you need to know your children. A child who is afraid of failure may at first practice for many days before he has enough confidence to volunteer for a test. This kind of child may sometimes be encouraged by having an oral practice test and, if necessary, a written practice test the next day, the emphasis always being on how many words he already knows.

Involving the Children   Explain to the children that you want to find out which words they already know how to spell. Then each child will only have to work on the words he needs to know.

When a child decides he is ready for a test he writes "Spelling," his name, and the test number on the chalkboard. If a child has extra words, words he has missed from a previous test, he puts a plus sign next to his test name and number: "Anna C6+." Anna missed "when" on C5 so she has been studying it along with her C6 words. Just be-

FIGURE 7.6   DATED RECORD CARD

Dec. 6	Mon.		Tues.	Wed.		Thurs.		Fri.	
Tina	T. B6	ate again	C1	T. C1		C2	take just	T. C2+	
Anna	T. C6	when	D1	D1		T. D1		D2	
Elaine	C6		T. C6	D1	does	T. D1+		D2	hold
Pam	C3		T. C3	C4		C4		T. C4	
Kathy	B4	any	T. B4+	B5		B5		B5	

fore lunch, one child copies the list on a sheet of paper and places it in the "spelling box" so it will not be misplaced. The teacher uses this list to organize her test cards and booklets for the next day. The spelling box contains all the test cards, the teacher record cards, the individual spelling booklets, any tests taken that day, and practice papers completed that day. Therefore, everything the teacher needs to plan for the next day is in one box.

Review Tests   Review tests should be given approximately every three to four weeks. All children who are working on a certain strip are given a twenty-word spot test on the preceding words which the teacher feels have caused the most trouble. For example, all children working on List C would have a test which includes words from List A and List B. A child must re-study any missed review words and subsequently pass a test on these words before he continues with his current spelling list.

Dictation   Dictation should be given once a week. Children are divided into two large groups. The groupings change as the children progress. Near the beginning of the year the children might be separated on the basis of whether they are working on their own spelling lists or still taking the group tests. Later on those children working on Lists A, B, and C might be placed in one group while those working on Lists D, E, and F are placed in another. Still later children working in state spelling books might be brought together for dictation.

Beginning with the least difficult list, dictate twenty spelling words per day. As you correct the tests place any misspelled or unknown word in the child's individual spelling booklet. As soon as a child has five or more words in his spelling booklet, he stops taking the group test. His name is recorded on the teacher's record card. He now studies the words in his individual spelling booklet. As soon as he has mastered these words he is given a test by another child or by the teacher. He places a star next to each correct word in his booklet. If all but one or two are correct, he moves his tongue depressor to the next pocket. This is his new list. He copies the list from the pocket, adds any word that was incorrect, and studies this list. When he is ready, he takes this test. Once again, any misspelled words are put in his booklet. If he has fewer than five misspelled words he may try for the next pocket. If he has five or more he must stay where he is until ready for the test on the words in his booklet.

Testing   Generally the children should sign up for a test a day in advance. They may, however, make an oral request at the beginning of the school day. We have two main reasons for advocating this procedure. First, it is an aid to teacher organization. It gives the teacher a chance to plan for the next day: to organize her record cards, to pull the test cards she will be needing, to decide who will do the testing, and to have the individual spelling booklets ready in case there is a misspelled word that will need to be recorded. Second, we feel the child who is tested a day after he has studied his words is more likely to remember those words in the future than the child who is tested immediately after he has finished studying his words.

Spelling Books   Our state issues one spelling workbook per child on a graded basis. In our program, these books are withheld until each child has mastered the basic vocabulary list appropriate for his grade level. Since children do not start this spelling book in September but are building their spelling and reading vocabularies in other ways, they are better prepared to read and follow the directions and to work independently when they receive the state spelling book. They also experience a great deal of success and are able to proceed through the books rather rapidly.

When a child receives his spelling book, he works independently, asking for help when it is needed. The books are divided into units, with five working units followed by one review unit. As a child completes a unit, he may either ask the teacher or another child to give him the unit test. The test may be oral or written. All tests are on tape and each unit test is followed by dictation or some other exercise appropriate to that lesson. A child may choose to take his test this way and be excused from group dictation. Review tests are given by the teacher or taken at the tape recorder. Four of our slowest second grade boys worked on their word lists until March or April. Since it was rather late in the year for them to begin working in a book, we gave them the option of continuing into the third grade list or receiving their book. Each one chose the book. They all loved it! They worked like beavers. Every spare minute they were working in their spelling books or taking a test. By the end of May one boy had completed the book and also finished the third grade vocabulary list. A second boy accomplished the same feat by the time the school year was over. The other two almost finished the book and both begged to take it home over the summer, which they did.

Taping a Spelling Test   When taping a spelling test, be sure to speak slowly and distinctly. Give the number and the word, use the word in a sentence, and then repeat the word. Clear and correct pronunciation is vital in order to avoid confusion resulting from words which sound alike. Allow sufficient time for the child to write the word before proceeding (I spell the word slowly to myself three times before saying the next word). The format for a taped Unit test follows:

> "This is the spelling test for Unit _____ in Spelling Book _____. If you have completed page _____ in the spelling book, you should be ready to take this test.
>
> "There are _____ spelling words and _____ review words, _____ words in all. If you have not numbered your paper, you may number as you go.
>
> "I will say the word. I will use it in a sentence. Then I will say the word again. If you need more time, press the STOP button. When you are ready to proceed, start the tape recorder again. At the end of the test, I will repeat the words so you can check your work. Number One: 'end.' [pause] 'This is the *end* of the line.' [pause] 'End.' [long pause] Number Two. . . .
>
> "Now check your work. Number One: 'end.' Number Two. . . ." [This time give only the number and the word.]

If the unit test is to be followed by dictation, the following format is used:

> "There will be _____ sentences for dictation. Listen to the whole sentence before you begin to write. Sentence number one. Listen to the sentence. 'He has a flag in his hand.' Write sentence number one. 'He has a flag in his hand.' [pause] 'He has a flag in his hand.' Sentence number two. Listen for the sentence. . . . Write sentence number two. . . .
>
> "This is the end of test number _____. Press the STOP button."

Occasionally we follow a unit test with an exercise other than dictation. A sample follows:

> "Today, instead of dictation, you will write some new words by changing the beginning sounds of some of the spelling words you have just written. There will be eight of these words. Number One. If you can write 'game' you can write 'blame.' Number One is 'blame.' [pause] 'Do not *blame* me.' [pause] 'blame.' [pause] Number two. . . ."

In our spelling books every sixth unit is a review unit. Each review unit in the second grade book involves forty-five words. However, for the taped test, thirty of the most difficult are chosen. The format is similar to that described for a unit test. There is no dictation.

Each review unit in the third grade book involves sixty words. All words are given. The test is divided into two parts, with thirty words to each part. The child may take Part 1 one day and Part 2 another day or he may take both parts at one sitting. The choice is his. The format follows:

"This is the test for Unit _____ in Book 3. Unit _____ is a review lesson. This test has sixty words. There will be no dictation. If you have completed page _____ in Book 3, then you should be ready to take this test.

"The test will be in two parts. The first part will include thirty words. The second part will include thirty words. You may take part 1 and then later take Part 2 or you may take Part 1 and Part 2 together. If you are ready to take the first part of the test, we will begin now.

"Part 1, Unit _____ has thirty words. You may number as you go. I will say the word. I will use it in a sentence. Then I will say the word again. At the end of Part 1 you will have a chance to check your work. Number One. . . . Now check your words. Number One. . . .

"If you are only taking Part 1 at this time, press the STOP button. If you are ready to continue with Part 2, we shall go ahead now. Part 2, Unit _____ has thirty words. You may number as you go. . . ."

Advanced Work A second grader who finishes Spelling Book 2 returns to the basic vocabulary list. Upon completing this he receives Spelling Book 3. Unfortunately these books must be purchased at a local department store with teacher money as the child has already used the one book allotted to him by the state. However, if a child goes to grade three with his teacher-purchased spelling book partially completed, we are generally able to confiscate his state-allotted Book 3 to use the next year for another child; but we then need to buy the first child a Book 4.

A third grader who has finished Spelling Book 3 is given a teacher-purchased Book 4, unless we are able to confiscate one as described above. We find that Book 4 requires more teacher supervision and guidance. However, by this time in the year, the other children are working along independently, requiring less teacher help, and so we are able to devote more time to the children in Book 4.

A second grader who has finished Books 2 and 3 is not given a Book 4. Instead, he is placed in a dictionary program. This program involves an alphabetized composition book, a dictionary, and the unit lists cut out of some old, partially used Book 4 spelling books. These children will concentrate on learning to spell the words, with an emphasis on their definition. We feel this is good preparation for the work they will be doing in Book 4 the following year.

A child who is working in the dictionary program works independently. He copies the Unit words from Book 4 into his composition book. He then looks up each word in his dictionary and copies the first definition next to each Unit word. On the following line he uses the spelling word in a sentence. When he finishes his entries, he studies his words and their definitions. The teacher checks his book. He then takes his test on the tape recorder. These tests differ from the others as the emphasis is on the meanings of words and no dictation is included.

A taping format for the dictionary program utilizing Book 4 follows:

> "This is the spelling test for Book 4, Unit 1. You have been studying the meanings of words. I will give you a definition and you will write the word. Sometimes I will give you an extra clue. If there is a word you cannot remember, leave the space blank and I will give you that word again after the test.
>
> "There are seventeen words in the test for Unit 1. If you have not numbered your paper, you may number as you write. Number One. Write the word that means a floor covering [short pause], a floor covering [long pause]. Number Two. Write the word that means. . . .
>
> "This is the end of Test 1 for Book 4. If there are any words you did not understand, come to me after you turn off the tape recorder and I will help you with those words. Turn off the tape recorder now."

ENRICHING OUR LIVES

Working with children has always been a joy, but leaving the front of the classroom to mingle with students has enriched all of our lives. We are truly interacting in a way that was not possible before. Being able to share the rewarding experiences and occasional disappointments with other adults is an added bonus. Do our children learn more than children in traditional situations? I don't know. I do know it is rare for a visitor to leave our room without commenting on how involved and happy our children are. We believe our boys and girls are vitally engrossed in the many-faceted aspects of learning. We further believe that this nation needs involved, happy children who are turned on to people and to learning.

CHAPTER 8

WORKING TOGETHER

Don Mack and Kay Kemp

This teaching team is responsible for sixty-five youngsters ranging in age from nine to eleven. The authors share with the reader the ups and downs of learning to work together while struggling to provide their students with the best possible program. Individualization to them means "tailoring the curriculum and the day's activities to the needs of each individual child according to his level of ability or interests, and forming ad hoc groups on the basis of these needs." A typical day is described in detail. Reading, spelling, and math programs are discussed, as well as techniques for keeping track of the multitude of activities that emerge.

Individualization of instruction is interpreted differently by different educators. Many feel that it means providing instruction for each individual child, accompanied by programmed materials which meet his needs. Others emphasize the importance of thinking of ways to individualize with many children involved in certain activities. This is commonly called "grouping for learning skills," and the children are organized in a homogeneous manner. The first definition, we feel, has validity but should more properly be called personalization of learning. The latter does not match our objectives because, as teachers who have worked with multi-ages for many years, we agree with current research which emphasizes random selection in class groupings. Our program is essentially nongraded, and this permits us to work with various ages but with many similar levels of comprehension and ability.

We believe that individualization of instruction means tailoring the curriculum and the day's activities to the needs of each individual child according to his level of ability or interests, and forming ad hoc groups on the basis of these needs. These groups may last anywhere from three to eight weeks. They meet by pre-arrangement or as the need arises. In the beginning, age was an important factor in the selection of students for these groups, but as we have become more knowledgeable about the possibilities of cross-age grouping and more sophisticated in our understanding of individualization, we have ceased to emphasize either age or ability. We are sold on the idea that nine-year-olds can easily work on the same level as eleven-year-olds, and sometimes they are physically as large or at least as able to take on similar physical tasks.

We are responsible for sixty-five youngsters who range in age from nine to eleven years. The two of us have been working together as a team for several years. We share with the rest of the staff a number of basic goals: to develop self-esteem and a better self-image in the child, to foster self-direction and self-motivation toward education, and to promote self-responsibility in the learner.

WORKING TOGETHER

The fact that we do work together as a team is basic to an understanding of our approach to individualization. It is difficult to assess or at times to recognize your own teaching style until you have another teacher around day after day—listening, observing, and helping. Even more important than the other person's suggestions or criticisms is the unconscious mirroring of your own teaching techniques, good or bad. Teachers who have taught alone for many years find it especially difficult at first to accept another teaching style or a figure of equal power in the same classroom. The professional façade of the ever-smiling, sweet-natured, even-tempered, popular teacher who never makes a mistake or raises his voice in front of the children is difficult to maintain on a daily basis. After a while, you find yourself lowering your reserve and beginning to resemble more closely the real person underneath the professional exterior. After a time, each of you begins to question his own teaching effectiveness and little comments are dropped: "Well, I'm sure that explanation was as clear as mud!" or "You do have a tendency to be verbose, my dear." Soon, teachers who work closely together begin to realize that large-group instruction is ineffectual and that directions have to be repeated as often and reviewed as frequently as they would be with individuals or smaller numbers. The more we read and see of the alienation of the young, in the news media as well as in our own classroom, the more we realize that an individual, humane approach to the dissemination of learning is a great deal more realistic and effective. The more we realize that children learn in different ways, the less we are concerned that instruction for all take place at the same time.

Teaching, then, for observant, sensitive team members becomes a professional and a personal experience. The team teacher is more apt to grow professionally and less apt to stagnate and become repetitious in his teaching routines. Also, because he comes into contact with one or more teachers who are vitally interested in improving the educational program, he feels the need to read more and attend university classes to become informed and up-to-date on the most recent educational innovations and practices. For the two of us, who had begun to feel ennui and a restlessness based on many long years in the same classrooms following much the same routines, and who had become increasingly concerned with behavior problems which seemed to multiply at a rapid rate, team teaching offered a new vista and an opportunity to attempt something different and challenging. So, making the decision to go into a team planning operation was simple. However, the decision was preceded by a year of discussion by the entire faculty. Implementing our program has been a four-year task of monumental proportions; and, while many things have been achieved, there is still a lot ahead of us.

One of the routine concerns at the outset was to decide with whom we wished to teach. It had been our experience that an association based on friendship is not usually workable or satisfying. Either the friendship or the teaching becomes more important—but one of them suffers. In fact, a stronger friendship may grow with someone who is different in personality and viewpoint because it must weather more storms in the beginning than a personal friendship would allow.

Those who think alike tend to solve problems alike while those who perceive things differently seem to have more alternatives and solutions available to them. The curriculum will probably be better balanced because it will reflect the concerns of both team members. One must have respect for the knowledge and ability of his colleagues. One must listen with a creative ear and be willing to change with grace. For example, one of us started out with the reputation for being fair but rigid. She is now considered to be the most permissive teacher on the staff. She lived with an image of the perfect teacher, based on childhood impressions, and was very aware that she could not live up to it. We both felt that there had to be a better way and agreed that we need not adhere to all the old puritanical edicts which obligated the teacher not only to teach the academic disciplines but also to be responsible for manners, dress, and decorum. Nevertheless, we were both edgy about sharing a classroom with another; but our eagerness to attempt the experiment overshadowed our doubts and reservations.

The first year was difficult because of physical limitations; we had two separate classrooms without connecting doors or a passageway. We found that the children tried to play us off against each other, separated as we were on and off throughout the day. However, when it came to a question of misunderstandings based on what we heard the children "quote," we soon learned to check these comments out carefully together!

One of us is not the least receptive to criticism but has a facility for easily and tactlessly criticizing others. And so we find it fascinating to observe how we have learned to deal with this necessary part of a successful team relationship. If the problem is minor, one says something to the other in a light vein. If, however, for her it is a serious criticism, she writes him a letter and hands it to him. If he has a severe criticism for her, he waits for a time when she's in a very good mood and then presents it as a mutual problem. We say all these things because, while this way may be unique to us, there *must* be a way that works for others. One must have a way to communicate with the other that is purposeful and does not allow for any withdrawal—no matter what!

We attribute much of the success of our program to our constant dialogue. Our planning periods most often result in "rap" sessions which give us an opportunity to address ourselves to the issues we feel are important to our team and the effect they will have on the children. It is not so much a question of dealing with general scheduling and planning as focusing on areas of the curriculum that are not working well for us, and more particularly on those students whose learning problems are causing them to be uncooperative and apathetic to our program. Often, when an issue of mutual concern is introduced in a team meeting, we spend time "brainstorming" until we are able to come up with another way or another direction to follow.

We do not emphasize the negative aspects of our program. We don't "nag" each other about what didn't work. Instead, we provide each other with a constant input of ideas, suggestions, and alternatives based on our reading and observation.

Whenever possible, we contact somebody who might have some information that would help us out. In the past we have relied heavily on the |I|D|E|A| research library with its wealth of literature dealing with all aspects of educational progress. We have taken an active role in the League of Cooperating Schools meetings whenever we have been able to attend. By participating in and conducting classes concerned with innovation and change, we have rechanneled our thinking many times.

We have never been apprehensive about experimentation. We share all kinds of new approaches, give a sympathetic ear to new ideas, and adapt those things which we feel might serve to implement and strengthen our progress.

GETTING STARTED

Each summer we spend a few days or even weeks of our time preparing for the first week of school. This involves planning initial activities for the new students, picking up the pieces for our former students (since our school is multi-aged, we always have a nucleus of students who return for a second and, in some cases, a third year to our team), and building in as many alternatives and choice opportunities as we can anticipate.

We decide the orientation process for the first day of the new school year. That is to say, we divide up the responsibilities for the opening of our program, deciding in advance who will present what information, explain certain routines, help guide the children to make decisions about their classroom environment, and so forth.

We prepare some pretest material for math and reading. Some of this material is of our own design, while some is selected from commercial sources available to us through district funds. Our selection and preparation are based on what we feel will best facilitate an evaluation of the students' performance.

We cover the bulletin boards with nonfading paper and decorate them with charts, posters, and pictures which have been laminated and which can easily be removed as the children begin to arrange their own room environment.

Orienting the Children

We begin by defining self-direction for them, and elicit comments and questions from them about what it means to them and how they can become self-directed. We discuss the importance of time in planning for one's learning. We also emphasize that assignment deadlines are determined by each individual's performance and are frequently very flexible. We encourage children to continue at a task until they are finished or sufficiently satisfied with their results to leave it for another time. We explain that the various groups will help us to keep track of their progress and their whereabouts throughout the day because we are accountable for these things as part of our job requirements. The children may have interruptions in their schedules which demand that they miss a group meeting. In this event, we only ask that they try to inform us ahead of time, and that they make arrangements to meet with another group in order to receive the necessary instruction. This is true also in cases of absence from school.

We give them time to arrange themselves where they like and with whom they wish. They may elect to sit at tables or desks or counters. They may store their possessions wherever room permits: in desks, in drawers, in the filing cabinet, on shelves, or in their individual mailboxes.

We explain the check-out board near one of the exits. Each child is given a square, flat wooden block with his name on it. On the board is a nail for his name block and above this storage area there are sections with other nails indicating the different places on the school campus where children may go for their learning: Discovery Room, Instructional Materials Center, County Library Branch (which is housed on our school campus), other classrooms to aide or tutor, errands, orchestra and chorus, or lavatories. The number of nails in each of these sections determines the number of students who may visit these areas at the same time. In cases where a speaker is appearing in the Discovery Room and the majority of the class wishes to attend, the name tags do not have to be used, as one of us will attend all or part of these events with the children.

At some time during the orientation we talk about materials and where they are stored. We also indicate that each child is responsible for the storage and maintenance of all materials and equipment in our classroom. The playground equipment may be checked out for each recess, but the child who takes out the equipment is responsible for its return. A sign-up sheet is posted near the ball cart for this purpose.

The involvement of the children in the initial decisions is manifold. Besides their opportunities for mobility within and without the classroom, decisions about their areas of the classroom, placement of their materials and belongings, and so forth, we also indicate that they will have many choices in the curiosity or interest groups that will be forming. Initially, the science and health groups are formed in this manner: A topic or question is placed on the board and those children who would like to engage in that activity may sign up for it. It might be:

Let's make a battery.
What are molecules?
Are all germs harmful?
Drug abuse.
Who wants to go on a fossil hunt?

Another area of decisions for them is what teacher they would like to work with in a given group situation. Often, this decision is changed by the student after the preliminary weeks of exposure to a particular teacher's style.

In the event of special assemblies, films, or activities of interest offered in the Discovery Room, the children have the option of attending or remaining in the room. No child is forced into any large group assemblage unless he decides that he would like to learn more about whatever is being discussed or viewed. His choices of involvement are endless, but his decisions about participation are his own.

Physical Facilities

Room arrangement is subject to change on a daily basis. (See Figure 8.1 for a diagram of a sample room arrangement.) It is dependent mostly on the youngsters' decisions and the physical needs of the groups. For example, a science or art activity might require a great deal of counter or floor space. When it is not performed on the outside patio, folk dancing requires pushing the desks around to provide an open area.

The first week we have some Interest Centers on the counters and a few games on tables. The Interest Centers display many manipulative devices. There are also practice and follow-up materials in these areas. The games which seem most popular and which we put out from the very beginning are: Bingtac (a multiplication or addition game), Thinker (a game of strategy and logic), Battleship, and Probe.

There is also an electric pencil sharpener and an electric typewriter for the children's use. These facilities and all of the other materials around the room are their responsibility, and the continued use of them is determined by the manner in which they are handled and maintained. If a child mistreats anything, it is removed until the missing parts are found, for a firm commitment has been made on his

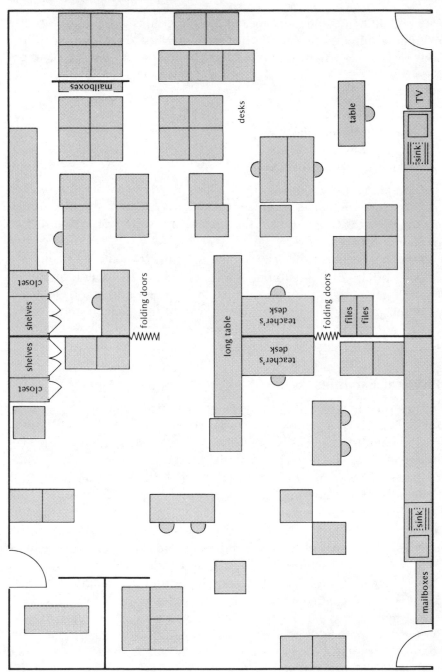

FIGURE 8.1   ROOM PLAN

part to use the material or equipment correctly. The same policy holds true for the name tags. If a child abuses the checking-out privilege or monopolizes certain areas outside the classroom, his name tag is removed from the board for a certain period (usually a week) and he is not allowed to leave the room without the permission of one of us.

The children soon learn by trial and error that their success and happiness in our open-structure team is largely determined by the choices they make and the alternatives for their behavior that they practice. It is a generative process in which the child evaluates himself constantly and performs according to his own needs. He learns quickly that self-responsibility is a very important element in the successful operation of his classroom.

Orienting the Parents

At all times we encourage the parents to visit, observe, and help in our classrooms. We invite parents by letter to visit us or inform them of any activity we are about to begin, especially if it is of a controversial nature. As a school we try to schedule an evening of Classrooms in Action in which we attempt to simulate some of our daily programs for the parents who are unable to visit during the day. Also, at the first opportunity we make very clear to them our policies about homework, and the importance of the child's involvement in the choice of activities for his program. We solicit their participation in the classroom, especially indicating our desire to have any parent or resource person who has a particular talent or skill that will enhance the learning process and make our program more vital and effective.

We contact the parent on the spot in the event of any serious *contretemps* in which his child is involved or any learning problem he seems to be experiencing. In this way, as well as through our open-door policy and the child's home reports about his school day, our public relations with our parents and their support of our program are confirmed.

KEEPING IT GOING
Preparation

Time organization is extremely important to consider—not only the students' time but the teachers' time as well. First, let us explain how we, as a two-man team, organize our time for instruction and preparation. An early agreement with the Board of Education and the superintendent provided our school with one minimum day per week for team planning. In order to acquire this precious time, we agreed to increase our dismissal time on the other four days of the week by ten minutes and to begin our daily classes five minutes earlier than the rest of the district. Prior to this agreement with the Board we simply had to find time to plan together—before and after school, on the weekends, during our lunch periods, breaks, etc. At any rate, we do have a long time block once a week in which to get together and do our decision making.

It is during this time that we decide who is going to take responsibility for leadership in all the areas of the curriculum. We have usually made some decisions individually about how we would like to proceed, and these are discussed, criticized, modified, or restructured at this time. For example, one of us may take leadership in Language Arts and have a plan for individualizing different levels for linguistic practice and composition activities. Perhaps several practice papers have been dittoed ahead, and, if we agree that they are meaningful, we will incorporate them into our lesson plan. In this way, if either team member is absent or called out for an emergency, the other member can step in and present the lesson and material, cognizant of the goals of the lesson and the procedure to follow.

Preparation time is also a daily thing except in cases of conflict with testing, field trips, assemblies, etc. We each enjoy a fifty-minute release time period in which to gather our materials, prepare lessons, type, and ditto. Often this time is spent right in our classroom because we need some of the children to help us with a project we are preparing or need to be near the other team member to discuss some ideas or work out a solution for an individual student problem. Other times we take this opportunity to visit other classrooms or observe activities in the Discovery Room or the Instructional Materials Center. When one of us is out of the classroom, we often have the assistance of an associate teacher.

A Typical Day

The students' time is organized as follows:

8:45—Roll call, lunch count, announcements. (The children put their names on the board if they are buying lunch. These are numbered, and a child makes a written copy for our desk so that we don't have to count bodies. In this way there are fewer arguments about who ordered what.) Roll call is simplified as we rely on the youngsters to tell us who is missing—they know who sits near them and are usually quite reliable. The typical minutiae of opening class ensues with announcements and reminders, flag salute, minutes from Student Council and Discovery Center Representatives meetings.

9:00 to 10:20—Language Arts: On Mondays, Tuesdays, and Thursdays the children write essays, choosing from a variety of topics. The length of the essays depends on each individual child; some will catch on quickly and write reams while others need more information and special help from one of us. At the same time, on these same days, a small group (no more than ten) is seated in a circle and encouraged to discuss topics from the health books. These groups consist of all ages, since the graded texts cover the same topics for all grades, being presented on a more sophisticated level for the upper grades. These groups continue to alternate until all the youngsters have had an opportunity to participate. It usually takes a month to accomplish this for all. In this circle they are permitted and encouraged to talk to each other and thus clarify their own knowledge, turning to the teacher only when the need is apparent.

9:30—One of us takes a small reading group to the special reading room.

10:00—One of several linguistics groups goes to the same room for a specific lesson in grammar. Those remaining in the room have free study time. The linguistics groups are arranged according to specific needs which we have identified in the composition papers. One group may work on syntax, another on punctuation, but each group works on only one specific skill at each fifteen-minute meeting. Thus, each group meets once a week and has a review quiz once a week or every two weeks, depending on the nature of the skill.

10:30 to 11:10—Math activities in this time block are described in the section on Math (page 158).

11:10 to 11:35—A limited-choice period. The students opt for spelling practice or handwriting drills. These can alternate every few days except for children who really don't need that much practice in handwriting. They may then continue spelling or have study time.

On the other two days of the week, Wednesday and Friday, we begin at 9:00 for a half-hour period with spelling, in which dictionary skills are introduced. Most of the class is involved in this activity except for those youngsters who belong to the school orchestra and those youngsters who are scheduled for some activity in the Discovery Centers.

11:35 to 12:15—Lunch.

12:15 to 1:15—The students return from lunch at 12:15 and prepare a written contract for the SDI (Self-Directed Investigations) period.

1:15 to 2:00—The aforementioned contract is evaluated for each child. Also, during this time small groups meet with one of us or with an associate teacher for science and social studies activities. These groups meet all over the place: the patio area, Instructional Materials Center, cafetorium, the neighboring park—any place that is serviceable or appropriate.

2:00 to 2:10—Recess.

2:10 on—P.E. classes on Mondays and Wednesdays; films on Thursdays. Once again, films are optional; those youngsters who do not wish to see the available film fare may use the period for study or research activities. Music on Fridays for those who have not made other arrangements. This last period is rather rigidly scheduled, but lack of space and equipment limits us.

Keeping Track

Conferences   Because we individualize our program, we are available to the youngsters needing "quick—right now" help. Therefore, they are able to find one of us for instant aid. Often, if we are engaged at the moment with another child or several children and a child requests help, we suggest that he ask a friend, check with another youngster involved in a similar activity, or wait until we are available and try to find something else to do in the meantime.

We make a point of speaking to each individual child several times every day to discuss an activity, future plans, or extracurricular occurrences, such as Little League, swimming, or ice-skating. On a more formal basis (concerning academic progress) it is probably three or four times a day that we contact each of approximately thirty youngsters, thereby covering the entire group of sixty-five. There is no predetermined plan in the sense that we decide who will contact which child. Rather, contact occurs naturally, according to the groups we teach.

Class Lists   Each year we type a dittoed alphabetical list of our children and line it off so that it looks like graph paper with space across the top to inscribe dates, chapter numbers, topics, or any other necessary notations for quick reference (Figure 8.2). We reproduce about fifty copies of these name lists, thus enabling us to have class lists available to us for keeping track of every subject area, group, and individual assignment. As we complete each page, we place it in our file for quick future reference, especially when parent conferences come up. Each of us uses these lists in his own particular way. After each progress report to parents concludes, we begin with fresh sheets for the next quarter. All of these documents are carefully filed away for our reference at any time until the end of the school year.

Records   Each child makes a personal commitment in the form of a contract (Figure 8.3). He also evaluates his work at the end of the contract period. These are carefully filed until progress reporting time. Prior to any reporting to parents, each child places all his papers which have been corrected or annotated by us in a folder along with his completed contract. He is totally responsible for keeping track of his own papers. It is now that our alphabetical lists come in handy and serve as reminders to us for all the papers we should expect them to have gathered. Most of the students' work is self-corrective. We permit them to use the Teacher's Editions to correct their math, spelling, and reading. In the event that an assignment is not taken from a text, the answers are written on the blackboard or a desk copy of the correct responses is made available to them. Formal quizzes are corrected by us or by students whom we designate.

Evaluation   Because we are "open structure," we have a scope and sequence of tasks in our instructional program. We have established minimum amounts of work to be accomplished by each child with our observations. We do not check cumulative record folders and the standardized test results inscribed within them. Our opinions are based on the pretests and the daily performance of the child in the classroom, as well as upon observations of each child and conferences with him. As teachers you will probably understand the various ways a child reveals his ability, which we are conditioned to observe: his handwriting, his conversation, his approach to his task, his ability to keep himself occupied constructively in the classroom, his rate of response in

FIGURE 8.2 CLASS LIST

Math—Tues. Test	2-1	2-8	2-15	2-22	2-29
Adams, Mary	16/20*	abs†	14/15		
Andrews, Sue	13/14	12/18	9/9		
Brown, Sharon	21/21	14/15	11/12		
Butler, Joan	21/21	6/9	13/14		
Byington, Ann	14/20	3/8	8/9		
Campbell, Patty	5/9	4/9	14/14		
Cleod, Val	6/12	9/10	13/18		
Edwards, Elaine	5/6	14/22	20/24		
Gladwin, Jane	11/11	16/18	13/14		
Hall, Susie	13/14	22/22	14/14		

*16 = number right
20 = number attempts
†abs = absent

Spelling—November–December	Unit	List	Test	Unit	List	Test	Review	Unit	List
Adler, Mark (Sp. Bk.)*	1-2		25/30	3	Sc. St. 14/20	20/20	25/25		
Andrews, Patrick (own)†		Sci 16/20	18/20		Sci 14/20		21/25		
Ayalla, Lee (own)		Sci 6/20	15/20		14/20	15/20	15/20		

Boardman, Phil (Sp. Bk.)	1–3		35/42	4–S		25/30	19/25
Bundy, Sam (own)		Hlth 15/15	abs		Sci 20/20		30/30
Carroll, Pete (Sp. Bk.)	6		50/50	F-8		21/21	25/25
Darby, Chuck (Sp. Bk.)	1–3		30/31	4–5		16/25	24/30
Denton, Mike (Sp. Bk.)	5–6		25/25	F		22/25	24/29

*Sp. Bk. = Spelling Book
†Own = selects own words from textbooks or other sources

Reading—January	Vocab.	Comp.	O.K.	Rdg. Game
Adams, Mary	√*	√	O.K.	Probe
Andrews, Sue				
Brown, Sharon				
Butler, Joan	X†	√	1/10	X
Byington, Ann	√	√	O.K.	Probe
Campbell, Patty	√	√	O.K.	X
Cleod, Val				

*√ = finished task
†X = didn't work on this

FIGURE 8.3   SAMPLE CONTRACT

My Wednesday contract is: To work on my health project	I will work: With Mary	I (was, was not) successful because: I finished the chart and wrote a paper explaining it.
My Thursday contract is: To read *Huck Finn*	I will work: By myself	I (was, was not) successful because: I enjoyed the two chapters I read.
My Friday contract is: To play "Monopoly"	I will work: With Joan, Sue, and Brenda	I (was, was not) successful because: I lost!
My Monday contract is: To make a ceramic pot	I will work: By myself	I (was, was not) successful because: I really like working with clay.

My evaluation of the week:
It was a pretty good week. I should have worked more on my health project. I will next week, though.

large- or small-group instruction, his creativity or ability to synthesize an idea and produce something new and original. All of these items contribute to our evaluation of the child's ability and our expectation of his progress.

THREE PROGRAMS

So far, we have discussed how we set up and maintain our classroom in rather general terms. In the sections which follow, we will attempt to explain our strategies for instruction in three subject matters, reading, spelling, and math.

Reading

Reading is usually uppermost in most elementary teachers' thoughts, not only in the fall, but throughout the school year. During the first few weeks of school we give a screening test which is usually somewhat standardized. The results of this test provide us with a grade-level placement for each child in the areas of comprehension, vocabulary, and speed–accuracy. We make it a policy to discuss the results of these tests with each individual child. We feel it is important to emphasize this last step. We let the child know his strengths and weaknesses as indicated by the test and ask him to help us make some decisions about what will be most effective in helping him to make progress. It is important that he be aware of our interest and concern for his success in order that he will be willing to accept the alternatives we have to offer him.

We explain that we are planning to organize several reading groups and that he will be invited to participate in one or more of them. The degree of his involvement will probably determine the kind of growth he can expect to make in the reading activity. We also emphasize at this point that his reading skills will be greatly advanced if he reads as often as he can and whenever possible, and that he should take advantage of the many reading books in our room and those available in the Instructional Materials Center and the County Libraries. We do not have homework as such, but the child is encouraged to read at least one hour in the evenings.

Even if your school has the advantage of a special reading teacher who is available to work with serious remedial problems, not all students will be able to receive this attention. Therefore, your students will have to make a serious commitment to function at the top of their potential in your existing reading program. In our school we do have a special reading teacher who has her own room. Since she has a double assignment and spends the afternoons at another school in the district, her room is vacant in the afternoons. Thus, we are able to make arrangements with her for the use of her room every afternoon for forty-five minutes of reading activities.

Because she was able to see the advantages of opening her special room with its variety of activities for the enrichment of our reading activities, our special reading teacher spent a great deal of time observing our classroom activities in order to determine the needs of a larger group of children than just those with whom she had contact each day. After discussing the situation with us, she decided to arrange her room as a lab, with stations for different skills and levels of ability. Using charts, she identified many of the word attack skill problems and provided follow-up materials to accompany them. She also devised games and related materials to help reinforce each concept and skill. What had been a comparatively exclusive reading program for a special few had evolved into a Reading Lab which was open for many and which became an integral part of our total classroom program.

In our classroom we also have a Reading Interest Center which contains a wealth of reading materials: puzzles, dictionary skill work, Reader's Digest Skill Builders, readers which contain short selections followed by questions, alphabet ladders (several variations of which were designed and constructed by our special reading teacher), the SRA Literary Sampler, and special skill cards dealing with context clues, inferences, and various word attack skills. We spend several class periods at the very outset carefully explaining and demonstrating each of these activities.

Based on the results of the pretests we form reading groups according to individual needs. Any youngster who scored below his own age level on the test is considered for placement in one of the groups which will regularly visit the Reading Lab. We deal with nine-, ten-, and eleven-year-olds, but the reading groups are not organized according to age levels. It is quite conceivable that an eleven-year-old could be working at the same level as a nine-year-old.

Only one skill is taught in each of the groups; therefore, a child who has difficulty with comprehension as well as word attack skills may be in two different reading groups each week. In order to avoid any "grade" labels or "top group–low group" stigmata, we designated each group with an Indian name:

Mohawk Group—concerned with vocabulary growth

Comanche—comprehension

Apache—listening and accuracy practice

Navajo—speed in silent reading

Delaware—at age-level expectancy or above, concerned with inference and interpretation

The first four groups use the Reading Lab alternately throughout the week. Delaware meets individually with the teacher in the classroom on certain days to read orally or discuss the reading activities in which each individual child had been engaged during the week. Each child knows which days to be prepared for this conference because he is classified according to the days of the week: Monday's Child, Thursday's Child, etc.

Here is the breakdown of all five groups:

Mohawk works with the Webster Word Wheels and the Category vocabulary cards. The former are checked with the teacher orally. The latter are self-corrective. Each child keeps a log folder which contains entries for each activity he engages in and his results.

Comanche works with the standard reading text booklets for silent reading practice. These are also self-corrective, and the score indicates the achieved reading level for each exercise.

Apache is given fast drills by the teacher as well as a listening test after the teacher has orally read a selection to the group.

Navajo is given practice drills in silent reading selections using many of the same materials as the Comanche group. The only difference is the accent on speed reading, since the selections are timed.

The *Delaware* group consists of about twenty-five youngsters. The children form their own smaller reading groups, which are composed of two to five members. Each group selects a book to read with the teacher. They meet with the teacher twice a week and spend thirty to forty minutes on reading. The teacher, or a group member, volunteers to read the story aloud. The teacher watches the children to see if they are comprehending the story line as well as the vocabulary (whether or not the teacher is reading, she can observe the children closely in such an intimate group). If a youngster does not understand the story or a particular word in it, he usually says so. Difficult passages or words are then discussed.

Each group member has a dictionary and each person may look up a troublesome word immediately. Occasionally a youngster offers a definition that is accurate, in which case the reading is continued without reference to the dictionary definition. The teacher keeps a notebook with pages designated for each day's group. Reading time, date, chapter being read, and problem vocabulary are recorded as well as any pertinent information indicating individual and group growth or needs. The group may select any book and may elect to change it for another at any time. In most cases the current book is completed. It is a pleasant time for all concerned and makes reading an event looked forward to by all.

Any student in any group which is not meeting at the time is welcome to use the Reading Lab and its materials and games. The only rule, imposed by the children themselves, is that their activities not interrupt the group which is regularly scheduled and convening at the time. Those who remain in the room are expected to find some activity from the Reading Interest Center or read quietly at their places. They may also take one of the reading games out to the patio on pleasant days if they wish. Because of the focus on skill practice and the amount of choice available to each child, the reading period is immensely pleasant and satisfying for everyone.

In the early spring we again test the entire group. Last year we reviewed the comparison of the fall and spring scores with each youngster. It was interesting to note that approximately 80 percent of the youngsters had progressed to their age-level expectancy or above as opposed to about 25 percent in the fall. The children were exultant and relieved. At that point we reshuffled the groups so that those who had made sufficient improvement were no longer involved in the remedial groups in the Lab, and those who had not made the expected gains were then included in the new groups.

Spelling

We have several objections to the California State Spellers. The two main objections concern the repetitious format of the spelling units and the proofread page in each section, which really reinforces error before the child has had an opportunity to master the words at the outset. We took instead four troublesome spelling problems and wrote them out:

1 "ei/ie" words

2 words that end in consonants ("When adding suffixes do you double the consonant or not?")

3 words that end in "e" ("When adding a suffix do you drop the 'e' or retain it?")

4 words that end in "c" ("Do you add 'k' and then the suffix?")

We presented a dittoed sheet with the rules and their exceptions to each youngster and included ten words representative of each rule, leaving a blank in the appropriate place: e.g., "rec__ve." The first week we discussed the rules with the entire class. The youngsters then were free to use their dictionaries to find the answers. We answered any individual questions.

The next week we made new lists of ten words each for each rule, this time instructing the children to use *only* the paper with the rules on it to solve their spelling problem. We did this, using the same four rules, for approximately five weeks. Not every youngster had to participate after the second week. If a child got seven out of eight words correct on a rule (or rules) we assumed he had understood the rules and could apply them when necessary. A few youngsters, of the total sixty-five, didn't need this and for them other arrangements were made. They played "Scrabble" or "Spill and Spell." They kept lists of each word they composed in the games and we looked the lists over each day and conferred with the "composer" if necessary to help correct spelling errors. The sixth week we composed lists (using the words from the first five weeks) of twenty words each as a review test. Eighty percent of the children did very well. The youngsters who did not do well received more individual attention and achieved some growth. These youngsters quizzed each other daily as we did. We also made crossword puzzles for them and held spelling "bees."

For the next six weeks we repeated this plan with four new rules and their exceptions:

1 words ending in "f" and "fe" that change to "ves" for *some* plurals

2 words that add "s" or "es" to form plurals

3 words that change form to become plural: e.g., "mouse—mice"

4 adding "s" to compound words: e.g., "sisters-in-law," "step-brothers," "vice presidents," etc.

The sixth week brought a review of this second set of rules. Then we changed the routine. This time we cooperated closely to integrate spelling with the language arts program. We gave weekly composition assignments. These we carefully checked, underlining any misspelled words. Once a week we collected words from the youngsters that they wanted to have on the spelling list from their misspellings in compositions. The youngsters chose partners and tested each other, then turned in the scores to us. This activity lasted approximately six weeks.

During the next six weeks we took abbreviations from a dictionary (twenty per week) and had the students look those up.

During the last few weeks of school, we gave each child a list of Latin roots (approximately ten at a time) with their definitions. The youngsters use their dictionaries to find two or three words to fit the definition. It is difficult for a few and so others help them out if we are unavailable.

Perhaps we should explain that we have formal spelling time twice weekly for a thirty-five minute period. Many youngsters work more than twenty minutes per day on their own and seek our help only when necessary.

Math

Our math program consists of a potpourri of methods supported by a variety of teaching approaches. We have become adept at finding ways to reach each child, as we use grouping for math only during the first few weeks, when we are following up on screening tests which we give the first week of school.

To form math groups initially, we use either standardized or teacher-designed tests. These tests start with the simplest level of knowledge, such as simple addition problems, and continue through complex percentage problems. Our teacher-constructed tests are limited to twenty-five or thirty items, to facilitate a rapid judgment of each youngster's immediate needs and levels of understanding. Together we evaluate the results of the screening tests, then discuss them with the youngsters, and then begin to form groups for certain skills.

These groups are flexible and overlapping, and many times we find that the students become proficient again in some of the skills they appear to lack after a brief review period, since they tend to forget over the summer hiatus unless they have had tutoring or summer school classes. Thus, the duration of the math skill groups depends on the students' progress and understanding of the concepts involved. A child is not asked to be in several groups at once; however, he may elect to join in on the next group if he so desires, even though he has not completed the work of his own group. At any one time, we may have one group working on addition and subtraction, another on multiplication, still others on division, fractions, measurement, and so forth.

As soon as the youngsters seem to have improved and have "caught up" on the review math, they are encouraged to go ahead on a completely individualized basis. Every Tuesday we distribute a twenty-minute teacher-made quiz which presents again the simplest problems and the most difficult and gives us a continuing profile of each individual child's progress. We require two pages of math a day; each page must have at least fifteen problems but no more than twenty. We have a paid aide who comes in each day and checks every paper that has been turned in. She puts only the number of correct problems at the top of the page. If seven or more problems are wrong she writes a "see the teacher" note, instead. As soon as she is finished with the papers we hand them out to the youngsters after we make notes to ourselves about which youngsters need help.

Record keeping for math is not terribly involved. The papers the children turn in are kept in a large envelope along with any checklists we have made of the group activities. On the front of the envelope is an alphabetical class list and opposite each name we write the date the work is turned in. It is easy to see at a glance who has not turned in their work and these youngsters are immediately contacted and/or reminded.

CHAPTER **9**

TEAMING FOR
INDIVIDUALIZATION

Janie Block and Flo Truitt

These two teachers share in the growth and development of seventy-five children, ages eight to twelve. They explain their approach to challenging and nurturing children with the major goal of effecting self-directed learners. Diagnosing, holding conferences, and evaluating to promote individualized learning in the language arts are discussed. Materials, room arrangements, scheduling of time, as well as the nuances of planning, criticizing, and sharing strengths as a team are explored.

Since our school has been a member of the League of Cooperating Schools, our staff has undergone a variety of changes. We have been freed from existing and accepted patterns of classroom philosophy and practice. We are daring where we were meek; we are decisive where we trembled; we accept failure as a part of change and learn from it; and we shout our successes loud and clear. We have become a vital, pulsating, "turned-on" group of people with a feeling of and for humanity.

But we didn't change overnight. Many hours were spent with leading educators concerned with innovation. We read voluminously from all the available research and spent a great deal of time in dialogue. And we hammered out a set of goals. Each child would become a self-directed learner within an atmosphere allowing him maximum growth. We would accept his specific strengths and weaknesses as a stimulus for creating a viable learning structure. We wanted to provide an environment in which each student could develop as a human being with a minimum of constraint and a maximum of freedom of choice. The child, we felt, is a complex organism with emotional, social, and intellectual needs which must be fulfilled. He comes to our classroom as a unique individual, and it would be our responsibility and opportunity to provide him with an environment which would sometimes challenge him, sometimes nurture him, and sometimes reassure him that he is a person of worth. We would strive to continuously expose him to the intellectual world around him. We would assume the right as professionals to diagnose what tools a child might need at a given time and to provide him with the opportunity to sharpen them, be it with a prod or a hug.

The first year the staff made several schoolwide changes. We opened the playground so that all children could play where they wanted and choose their own games, and sit and eat where they wished at lunchtime. We also made the library available to children whenever they needed it, rather than observing the traditional weekly hour. We asked parent volunteers to staff the library, to further open the choices available to children. And we added widely to the resources available to each classroom for the reading program.

Meanwhile, at the classroom level teachers began to individualize their reading programs, moving slowly away from the traditional three-group arrangement. This evolution to individualization was jerky and uneven. From a concurrent attempt to introduce an individualized math program on a schoolwide basis we were learning that effective changes are not always easy to bring about. For example, the homogeneous ability grouping of students was set up with the expectation that children would move freely from one group to another as their testing indicated. But in reality most stayed put; only about 10 percent seemed to change groups.

We also began the effort of team teaching. But at first this, too, was unproductive and frustrating. Our teams of four or five were too large to plan and interact meaningfully for their 140 students. Some of us began to see the inherent difficulties in being able to know that many children well enough to recognize them as individuals with learning styles uniquely their own. Applying this insight, we continued to change our organizational structure until we arrived at one in which we felt we could meet the needs of the individual child.

OUR OWN PROGRAM: GETTING IT STARTED

The two of us who are writing this chapter felt that we could meet the needs of the individual child best through a two-man teaming situation. We felt that teaming would provide us with the stimulation of planning together, criticizing and evaluating each other's teaching techniques, and sharing strengths and diverting problems. Furthermore, this arrangement gave the children an opportunity to relate to more than one adult.

We chose a multi-age group and were assigned seventy-five children ranging from eight to twelve years of age—that is, grades four through six. We felt that this plan would allow for greater flexibility in skill groupings. And there were other advantages as well. Having a wide range in the classroom provided us with older children who could serve as models for the younger ones. Also, an immature older child could interact with younger children with impunity and an aggressive young child could benefit from being in a group with older children. Leadership, intellectual discourse, and physical interplay could flourish regardless of age. We hoped a family atmosphere would develop and would encourage the responsibility, respect, and fondness which is often inhibited in the biological family because of sibling rivalry and other family pressures. And, we hoped it would be fun.

How To Spend a Summer

Our planning began as soon as the children were assigned to us. It was a summer of togetherness—we met many times and brainstormed. We pooled our materials and familiarized ourselves with our combined collection of resources. From our previous experience we decided that as we were getting to know the children by observing, holding conferences, and interacting, we would need to diagnose in the area of language arts skills. Some of the priorities of skills were word recognition, word meaning, comprehension, application, and synthesis. To that effect we used the district-provided follow-up and all other tools for skill follow-up which we had amassed. We put these into files according to major skill areas and labeled them as to degree of difficulty. When we were finished, we had files labeled "main idea," "character analysis," "vocabulary development," "capitalization," "homonyms," "synonyms," "antonyms," "outlining," "dictionary skills," "encyclopedia skills," "literary techniques." We also assembled and filed many word games such as Scrabble, Spelling Baseball, crossword puzzles, and anagrams.

While we were selecting and classifying, we did a great deal of talking to each other. We concurred that we needed to set up ways to guarantee that we both had teaching contacts with all the children. We wanted to see a child in more than one dimension. We wanted to be able to check out each other. To this effect we tentatively decided that each child would be a member of a skill group, which would be formed according to needs diagnosed by commercial tests, and that each child would be a member of a spelling group and a linguistic (grammar) group. We also agreed that written skills would be diagnosed and taught as needs arose from written work, such as stories. These groups would be temporary in nature and would meet only until the needed skill was mastered.

We discussed how we would handle written expression. We wanted to encourage creative writing, but the thought of reading seventy-five stories daily or weekly was overwhelming. We felt obligated to react to what the children wrote, to give them feedback, and to help them in areas of need. We arrived at the idea of keeping diaries. Each child would make a daily entry, the choice of what he wrote being his—stories, puzzles, random ideas and thoughts, poems, feelings, etc.

An area of concern during our planning was that of room arrangement. While our room arrangement was not ideal for team teaching, at least we had adjoining classrooms. The door between them would be removed and effectively "lost" by our school custodian. We decided that one of the rooms would be arranged in such a way that the total group could meet there comfortably and that the other room would have most of the learning centers and function more as a work area. We purchased some thirty yards of carpeting and began to scrounge couches. We realized that seventy-five children needed more than one reading corner, so we provided two "mini-libraries." We arranged for a math corner filled with number games, puzzles, and manipulative objects; an audio-visual corner stocked with tapes, records, and filmstrips; and a science working and display corner. We manipulated furniture so that there was room for small-group teaching in both rooms. (See Figure 9.1 for room diagram.)

And we collected materials:

Loads of books gathered, borrowed, purchased—whatever ingenuity could provide. Range of difficulty from very easy to adult books.

Magazines, pamphlets, manuals, travel folders, discarded high school textbooks, newspapers—anything with print and pictures.

Games, both commercial and teacher-made. Word games, puzzles,

Scrabble, Spill and Spell, dittoes mounted, dittoes run off—the criteria were variety and range of difficulty.

Couches, rugs, pillows, easy chairs—anything to make the rooms look less institutional and feel more comfortable.

Posters, pictures, paintings, quotations—anything to stimulate visually and intellectually.

Our First Day

We were really prepared for the first day! We had enough materials to sink the Titanic and were organized enough to launch Mariner 58, but as the bell rang we looked at each other and admitted to being nervous. Seventy-five children seemed like an awful lot! We gathered them all in one room on the large rug and told them what we were all about. We explained that we were a class of seventy-five meeting in two rooms with two teachers. We shared with them our reasons for thinking this organization was preferable. We explained the benefits to them: more individual help, more freedom of movement, two teachers to whom to relate, each with different experiences and different strengths, many different interest groups in which they might want to participate, a variety of learning centers, and, finally, the chance to have more friends in a family grouping. We also spoke of our personal motivation. We explained that we enjoy working together, planning and sharing ideas, and solving problems.

We imposed no rules other than those of basic human decency, consideration for others, commitment to self, completion of tasks, and respect for the common good. Without articulating it, the children felt free to do the necessities without permission, such as sharpening pencils, going to the bathroom, getting drinks, and going between rooms.

The children seemed quite delighted, and we began getting to know each other. We two teachers role-played. We pretended we had never met and wanted to get to know each other. We used interviewing techniques to the delight of the children and listed categories of questions on the board as we went along. They then chose someone they didn't know to interview. They also colored in a blank paper doll to depict the child they had interviewed. This provided an icebreaker as well as an immediate bulletin board. It also served as the first creative writing experience and gave us material to diagnose skills needed.

FIGURE 9.1   ROOM DIAGRAM

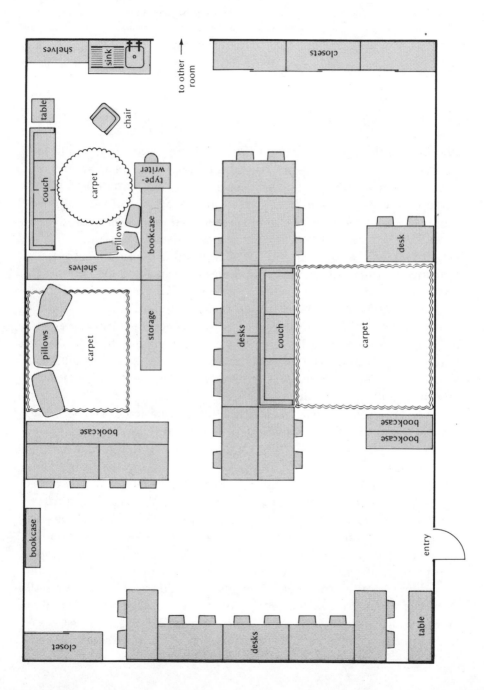

FIGURE 9.1 ROOM DIAGRAM (CONTINUED)

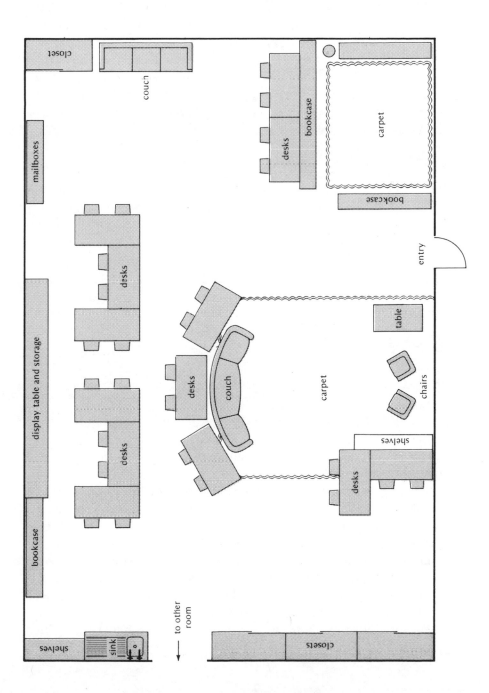

From this, our first language skill groups evolved: capitalization, punctuation, run-on sentences, incomplete sentences.

The next hour we initiated our reading program. We introduced a simple weekly calendar (see Figure 9.2) and instructed the children to record what they accomplished after each activity. This calendar was to be kept by the child for the complete week, at which time it would be collected, circled, and filed. If in a given area a child had a minimal experience, a conference was to be set up to discuss the matter. Commitments would then be made as to future activities in that area and teacher direction given when necessary.

FIGURE 9.2   WEEKLY CALENDAR

	Reading and Projects	Spelling and Language	Social Studies– Science	Math	Independent Study and Other Work
Monday					
Tuesday					
Wednesday					
Thursday					
Friday					

We taught a directed lesson on how to find a book in the minilibraries we had set up. Such skills as knowing the card catalog–Dewey Decimal system, author, title, and subject cards, etc., were taught and continued for the next two weeks.

Reading folders were distributed to each child. They consisted of a list entitled "Ways to Share a Book,"* a place to list books read, and a place to note new words found in the reading. The children were committed to reading one book per week, shared if they wished, and to finding three new vocabulary words from their reading. They then chose a book, listed it in their reading folder, and read for a while. This gave us the opportunity to hold conferences and to help those children who had difficulty in finding a book.

At the end of the hour, we gave a diagnostic spelling test, which

* See Chapter 3, Appendix A, for 49 ways to make creative book reports.

accompanies the spelling books used in our district. This gave us the opportunity to evaluate spelling ability regardless of grade level.

By the end of the Language Arts period, each child was reading a book and finding new words, had completed a directed library skill lesson which he corrected after completion, had filled in a record sheet of achievement, such as the name of the book he had chosen, had taken a spelling test which permitted us to place him in a spelling group the following day, and had been asked to bring in a spiral notebook which would be used as a diary. Each child also had met at least one new child and had had a writing experience as well as an art experience (the paper doll).

The First Weeks

During the next two weeks we rounded out our program by continuing to conference, giving directed library skill lessons, and administering reading and linguistic diagnostic tests.

Each day we introduced some new activities that the children might choose. We set up listening and viewing centers dealing with stories presented audio-visually. We presented word games, such as teacher-prepared and commercially produced crossword puzzles, which the children emulated with great success; scrambled words to be unscrambled, rebuses (a combination of words and pictures); finding words in arrays; Spelling Baseball, using current words; Hinky-Pinky (two rhyming words to a definition such as "plump feline"–"fat cat"), Anagrams, Scrabble, Authors, and so forth.

Some children who requested a class newspaper formed a group and with the help of a parent-aide they began working on the first issue. So successful was this group that it continued throughout the year with a rotating staff.

We were fortunate enough to have a parent trained in leading discussions of *Junior Great Books* and children who showed capability and desire were invited to join, provided they made a commitment to complete the series.

Manned by parent volunteers, our school library was open all day. Children who needed to choose or return a book could go at their leisure.

By the end of the second week, we had organized skill groups based on diagnostic tests and conferences so that we had evolved eight reading groups, each group meeting once a week on a designated day to practice a specifically needed reading skill with one or the other of us; seven spelling groups consisting of a remedial group which met daily, two groups that met twice a week, four groups that met once a week; three linguistic groups meeting every third day; language skill groups that met for a specific purpose when a need arose, such as practice in capitalization, punctuation, letter writing, etc. For those children who needed immediate gratification, we prescribed commercially produced reading programs which allow a child to read, complete, and correct the assigned work at one sitting. Added to this were the many and varied "choice activities" described earlier.

Involving the Parents

We called a parents' meeting the second week of school. We needed parents' support for the notion of having a class of seventy-five; and we needed their help in the classroom. The meeting was attended by most of the parents, all curious and concerned. We explained our program, answered many questions, and sought their help. Parents of older children were concerned as to why their children had been placed with younger children, and some concern was shown as to how we could get to know so many children. We explained our diagnostic procedures, expressed our concern for the individual, and delineated what we felt to be parents' responsibilities in regard to school. We asked for volunteers and for couches! The end result was a parent-aide group of two mothers per morning, ten in all, to work with individual children, helping them with spelling and reading, organizing small interest groups such as the newspaper, and sometimes just being a warm body to which to relate. We also received two couches and a beautiful cabinet for storage, as well as four table legs for which we have found no use to this day. The meeting engendered a feeling of warmth and togetherness and we decided to have more such meetings during the course of the year. This we did.

OUR PROGRAM TODAY

We now have a two-hour block for Language Arts. Each morning all seventy-five of us meet together and plan the day. At the end of the planning session (about fifteen minutes) the board will look something like this:

Reading	Spelling	Language	Conference
Read your book	David's group	Diary	Elaine
Vocabulary words	Scott's group	Foxy Function	Geri
Magic Word meets		Janet, Val,	Sandy
Satire group meets		Eddie, Mike B.	Carol
Propaganda		Red Roberts meet	Bill
Mike, Bob,		Capitalization	Nancy
Scott, Barbara		Mark, David,	Sam
Newspaper		Katrina, Susan	Debbie
group—get	*Library*		
articles in	Val		
Junior Great Books	Geri		
meets	Danny		

Each child has his weekly calendar on which he is expected to note what he has accomplished in the various areas. The first heading is Reading. Each child knows he is expected to read approximately one book a week. He may share it with the class or a small group if he so desires. In practice it is a rarity to have a book shared with the whole class; most sharing is done with small groups in one of the mini-libraries.

Other possibilities for reading include the *Junior Great Books* group, the newspaper group, and many games referred to earlier. In addition, each child meets with his skill group once a week. He also may be involved in an enriching reading experience such as reading and discussing *Brave New World* or *Candide*. He may get involved in a group discussion about a book read by a number of children or he may join a discussion about a particular literary style. Right now we have a group interested in puns and another immersed in satire. Each day different groups meet and each day the planning board looks a little different. Building vocabulary words is an ongoing activity. All of these activities are listed on the planning board under Reading.

The second heading is Spelling. In that listing are usually two groups, one meeting in each room for a teacher-directed lesson, which includes a test on the unit completed and an introduction to the next unit. Some groups meet once a week, others twice, and a remedial group meets daily. Children who were absent when their group met have the responsibility to ask for a makeup test which is then given by the parent-aide. A child may choose to do all his spelling in one day or a little each day. By and large the spelling groups maintain a stable membership, insofar as we feel the spelling program serves to teach patterns of words which can be applied to their words ad infinitum, rather than learning twenty words per week, which are soon forgotten. The need to change books is then not present. The sole function of the book is to give experience in following directions and completing a task independently.

The third heading is Language. A linguistic group which is unchanging meets every third day and is listed on the planning board. The diary is listed as a reminder; and perhaps a specific writing skill group will be meeting for those who need or want it. This group may function for one lesson only or may have a return engagement if the need is demonstrated. Word games may be listed, and those who want to play will volunteer. By and large the players will volunteer only if they have free time.

Another heading is Library. The children who need to go may sign up, check out books as they see fit, and return to the classroom, crossing out their names to show that they have returned.

The last major listing is Conference. Each child is asked to have a conference at least once a week. To be sure no one has been overlooked we keep a chart posted which each child marks to show with whom he has held a conference. It may be with either of us or it may be with a parent or an associate teacher.

Our conferences are multi-purpose. They may be requested by the child to talk about a book, just to chat or talk about problems, to discuss other classroom activities, to share something he has written, or to read to us. A conference may be requested by one of us for the same purposes. Every third week we focus on specific areas in reading such as plots, characterization, settings, or literary styles, and discuss these with the child.

Our groupings, then, can be voluntary, such as those formed for word games, the newspaper, or *Junior Great Books,* or assigned, such as those formed for reading skill, spelling, and language.

After we have planned on the board together, the children go to their cubbyholes where they keep their materials and choose what to do. Our pattern has evolved so that we have conferences for approximately the first half hour, then begin skill groups. We call the groups together as we planned on the board. As work is assigned, the children are asked to place it in a designated basket. If assigned work is missing, the following day a reminder of overdue work is posted on the planning board. The child is expected to make wise choices in his use of time and to fulfill his commitments—the hows and whens are individual choices. Work is returned via individual mailboxes.

We have found that most children make relatively wise choices most of the time. The ones who cannot, we help. Our help has consisted of a group named the Task Force, made up of those children who, either by teacher observation or by self-evaluation, have difficulty making choices and completing a task. The Task Force meets immediately after planning and sits down with one of us to decide what they are going to do first. When they have completed the initial task, they return to plan the second task, and so on for the morning. The aim is to allow the children to learn to list the tasks and complete them independently. The membership of the Task Force has shifted considerably as boys and girls become more independent and more decisive choice-makers.

CONSTANT EVALUATION

Boys and girls keep their own records. As previously noted, they maintain a weekly calendar, which allows them as well as us to see at a glance what they have been doing. They also record names and authors of books read, as well as a rather extensive vocabulary list. Their diary is a continuous record of their growth during the year. We check diaries weekly. They also have folders of completed work.

We, on the other hand, keep records of skill work, spelling tests, vocabulary and writing skills, as well as the record of conferences. (A sample form supplied to parent-aides is shown in Figure 9.3.) We each keep a grade book with all seventy-five names listed, in which we note results of diagnostic tests, pre- and post-tests, and mini-tests. The grade book entries complement each other.

Our evaluation is continuous and ongoing. We are always in the process of evaluating progress. The tool may be a spelling test or the diary; it may be a conference about a book or a conference at which a child tells us how he feels about himself or school; it may be formal or quite informal, but it is the basis of all planning for future skill development and activities. We have asked the children to evaluate their own progress twice a year. We have found them to be remarkably insightful and honest. We have also asked them to evaluate our program and have used this evaluation to make indicated changes.

Date _____

Dear Parent-Aide:

Today you will be working with the following children:

Student	Task	Notes
Mary John Melody Danny	Re-teach words missed	
Bill Steve Diane Carol	Blue Roberts p. 116 Help to understand adjectives	
David Doug	Read orally	

Please keep some notes. Jot down what you did and what subsequent needs the children have.

FIGURE 9.3   PARENT-AIDE FORM

The children, parents, and we have loved what we are doing. As a group and individually we continue to evaluate, change, add, and delete as seems indicated to make our program meet the goal of producing a self-directed learner who is aware of his responsibility to himself and to the rest of his society.

A SELECTED BIBLIOGRAPHY ON INDIVIDUALIZING INSTRUCTION

SECOND EDITION*

Lillian K. Drag

PREFACE TO THE SECOND EDITION

Since 1968, when this bibliography was first issued, there has been a definite trend away from the traditional closed classroom to the more open-structured model of individualization. In order to bring the list up to date, we have included many more titles on open education and added a new section on the environment needed to provide for more personalized learning.

Part I gives an overview of individualized instruction in which books and pamphlets are annotated and magazine articles are not. A few pertinent periodicals are listed. Materials related to the British primary schools are included in this section. Part II lists materials on individualization in the various subject areas, arranged by subject area. Part III is a compilation related to tactics and strategies for individualizing instruction. This part is subdivided: Section A includes nongrading and continuous progress. Section B, a new section, is on school environment: learning centers, open-plan schools, facilities, and affective environment. Section C covers grouping, flexible scheduling, and team teaching, and Section D, computer-assisted and programmed instruction. Part IV lists films; Part V, audio tapes. Needless to say, many of the titles in any one part may have useful information pertaining to another.

* The first edition of this bibliography was published by the Institute for Development of Educational Activities, Inc. (|I|D|E|A|), July 1968.

PART I. GENERAL REFERENCES
Books and Pamphlets

Alexander, William M., ed. *The Changing Secondary School Curriculum: Readings.* New York: Holt, Rinehart and Winston, Inc., 1967.
Galen Saylor writes on "What Changes in School Organization Will Produce Better Learning Opportunities for Individual Students?" and Chapter 10 is devoted to "Provisions for Individual Differences."

———— and Vynce A. Hines. *Independent Study in Secondary Schools.* New York: Holt, Rinehart and Winston, Inc., 1968.
Describes characteristics of independent study, as surveyed in selected schools, looking at achievement of pupils, spread of practices, and reaction of participants. Teacher skills, facilities, problems, and values involved are considered.

Almy, Millie. *Young Children's Thinking: Studies of Some Aspects of Piaget's Theory.* New York: Bureau of Publications, Teachers College Press, Columbia University, 1966.
A longitudinal study of children's thinking in which sixty-five children were studied successively in kindergarten and first and second grades. Replicates some of the lines of investigation used in Piaget's classical studies to study effects of classroom experience on the young child's thinking about natural phenomena. Findings imply that the teacher who has mastered Piaget's techniques will become more diagnostic and much more skillful in pacing instruction to the individual child's apparent maturity and rate of learning.

American Association of School Administrators. *A Climate for Individuality.* Statement of the Joint Project on the Individual and the School. Washington, D.C.: the Association, a department of the National Education Association, 1965.
Significant pamphlet which indicates there is a vast difference between "nurturing individuality" and "taking care of individual differences." Makes a case for American commitment to the individual human being in support of providing conditions of a climate that stimulates everybody's growth. Summary chapter offers concise guideposts for school and community which may be helpful as a checklist in self-evaluation.

Anderson, Robert H. *Teaching in a World of Change.* New York: Harcourt, Brace and World, Inc., 1966.
As basis for discussion, Anderson presents a three-sided view of teaching: pedagogy, knowledge, identification. An overview of the organization of schools is followed by specifics on theory and practice in the nongraded school and in team teaching. Paraprofessionals, the changing American schoolhouse, and the library-centered school are also discussed.

Ashton-Warner, Sylvia. *Teacher.* New York: Bantam Books, 1963.
Paperback edition of popular work of the artist/teacher describing

her years of teaching in a New Zealand infant school using the "key vocabulary" of individual children to facilitate their learning.

Association for Supervision and Curriculum Development. *Human Variability and Learning: Papers and Reports.* Fifth Curriculum Research Institute, edited by Walter B. Waetjen. Washington, D.C.: the Association, a department of the National Education Association, 1961. George Denemark's introduction notes two ways of looking at human variability: as the source of problems which one should seek to eliminate, and as an important resource which should be utilized most effectively. Six areas of differences are discussed: perception among individuals; types of intelligence; maturity level; rate of maturation; societal demands; and objectives for learning among both teachers and students.

————. *Individualizing Instruction.* 1964 Yearbook, edited by Ronald C. Doll. Washington, D.C.: the Association, a department of the National Education Association, 1964.
Treats the topic from the standpoint of discovery and release of potential in learners. Emphasizes the necessity for a close pupil–teacher relationship rather than organizational aspects of classroom or school.

————. *A New Look at Progressive Education.* 1972 Yearbook, James R. Squire, chairman and editor. Washington, D.C.: the Association, a department of the National Education Association, 1972.
A study of the ways in which the ideas of progressive education are once again coming to the fore. James Macdonald's introduction spells out some of these ideas: the concept of experience, the cultivation of individuality, purposeful activity, process, the curriculum as environment, freedom, and the social conditions of learning. Barbara Biber's "The 'Whole Child,' Individuality, and Values in Education" shows that these ideas *do* remain viable at the present time.

————. *Nurturing Individual Potential: Papers and Reports.* Seventh Curriculum Research Institute, edited by A. H. Passow. Washington, D.C.: the Association, a department of the National Education Association, 1964.
Presentations draw on psychology, psychiatry, and sociology to examine aspects of factors affecting the nurturing of individual potential. Passow discusses common threads: (1) each learner's uniqueness affects his interaction with teacher, peers, and curriculum, and this interaction in turn affects the total experience of the student and the extent to which he develops his potential; (2) some aspects have not been explored thoroughly in program planning and must be considered: the teacher's behavior and its consequence in terms of students' motivation, processes of creativity, teaching style, developing different kinds of intellectual abilities; (3) many sources of talent potential are still untapped or inadequately de-

veloped; (4) the complexity of interacting forces which stifle or unleash individual potential.

―――. *Removing Barriers to Humaneness in the High School*. Edited by J. Galen Saylor and Joshua L. Smith. Washington, D.C.: the Association, a department of the National Education Association, 1971. Position paper presented by James B. Macdonald, "A Vision of a Humane School," is examined and evaluated by other conferees. They identify some major barriers and discuss ways in which schools could "break out of the box." James Foley's "Teaching and Learning in the Affective Domain" describes teaching techniques used to create conditions of mutual respect and cooperativeness. Fred Wilhelms designs a curriculum.

Barth, Roland. *Open Education and the American School*. New York: Agathon Press (distributed by Schocken), 1972.
Describes an attempt to introduce open classrooms through the standard pattern of innovation from the top down. Indicates that reforms imposed by outsiders are often unsuccessful.

―――― and Charles H. Rathbone. *A Bibliography of Open Education*. Cambridge, Mass.: Education Development and Advisory Center for Open Education, 1971.
"An extensive resource which will assist further exploration," divided into Books and Articles, Films, and Periodicals, with publishers' addresses given.

Bassett, G. W. *Each One Is Different: Teaching for Individual Differences in the Primary School*. Armidale, New South Wales 2351: Australian Council for Educational Research, 1963. A conference report which summarizes much of the thinking that has been done on individualization of instruction, the nongraded school, and ability grouping.

―――. *Innovations in Primary Education*. New York: Wiley & Sons, 1970.
The author's report of recent developments in primary education in England and the United States affords the reader a rare opportunity to stand off and look at what is happening through the eyes of a wise and experienced educator. His discussion centers on educational objectives, modern developments in both countries, and the process of innovation in each. Excellent references are provided.

Beggs, David W., III, and Edward B. Buffie, eds. *Independent Study: Bold New Venture*. Bloomington: Indiana University Press, 1965.
Describes successful independent study practices and the nature of independent study, the goals of self-assumed learning activities, and the ways schools can organize to initiate a program. Chapters 3–6 make liberal references to specific school programs. Chapter 12, "The Administrator's Role," will help the school principal who wishes to foster change.

Blackie, John. *Inside the Primary School*. New York: Schocken Books, 1971.

A former Inspector of Schools in Great Britain interprets the findings of the Plowden Report, *Children and Their Primary Schools,* and cites specific examples in different subject areas to illustrate practice. A classic on open schools, now available in paperback.

Block, James H., ed. *Mastery Learning: Theory and Practice.* New York: Holt, Rinehart and Winston, Inc., 1971.
With selected papers by Peter Airasian, Benjamin S. Bloom, and John B. Carroll. Assumes that all students can learn well and offers relevant supporting research.

Borton, Terry. *Reach, Touch and Teach: Student Concerns and Process Evaluation.* New York: McGraw-Hill, 1970.
Describes the Affective Education Research Project in the Philadelphia public schools and his own experiences in it. Gives specific examples of practice and details on workshop experiences.

Brearley, Molly, ed. *The Teaching of Young Children: Some Applications of Piaget's Learning Theory.* New York: Schocken Books, 1970.
The difficult theoretical ideas of Piaget, Susan and Nathan Isaacs, and Jerome Bruner have been woven into examples of good classroom practice based on a unifying genetic psychological approach. Areas covered: science, art, literature, movement, mathematics, music, and moral education.

———— and Elizabeth Hitchfield. *A Guide to Reading Piaget.* New York: Schocken Books, 1967.
Presents seven major works of Piaget through excerpts describing methods of the original investigations. Brief comments at the end of each section indicate the teacher's role in using Piaget's findings, emphasizing the importance of helping children consolidate concrete experiences before mental operations and causal relationships occur. Stresses the match that is needed between the child's inner cognitive organization at each level and the appropriate school encounters to help develop the child's intellectual functioning.

Brown, Mary, and Norman Precious. *The Integrated Day in the Primary School.* New York: Agathon Press, Inc., 1970.
Two Leicestershire "Heads" provide practical help in everyday activities, organization, materials, etc., based on their own extensive experience.

Bruner, Jerome, ed. *Learning about Learning: A Conference Report.* Washington, D.C.: U.S. Office of Education, 1966.
Especially pertinent is Chapter 1 on inducing a child to learn and sustaining his attention, with contributions by Robert Sears, Jerome Kagan, Pauline Sears.

Cazden, Courtney B. *Infant School.* Newton, Mass.: Education Development Center, 1969.
An interview with Miss Susan M. Williams, director of the Gordonbrock Infant School in London, the school filmed by Lillian Weber (see Part IV: Films).

Darrow, Helen F., and R. V. Allen. *Independent Activities for Creative Learning.* New York: Bureau of Publications, Teachers College Press, Columbia University, 1961.
No. 21 of the series *Practical Suggestions for Teaching* encourages independent study to satisfy the child's interest and requires that he make his own choices from a variety of interest centers.

Drucker, Peter F. *The Age of Discontinuity.* New York: Harper & Row, 1968.
Sees school failure resulting from refusal to let children learn at their own pace. Makes a plea for more tools to help individualize instruction, pointing out that individual learning styles can differ as widely as physical differences.

Education U.S.A. Special Report. *Individualization in Schools: The Challenge and the Options.* Arlington, Va.: National School Public Relations Association, 1972.
Describes eight major systems for individualizing. Includes results of U.S. Office of Education study of forty-six schools using individualized instruction.

Educational Testing Service. *New Approaches to Individualizing Instruction.* A Report of a Conference. Princeton, N.J.: the Service, 1965.
John I. Goodlad's presentation "Diagnosis and Prescription in Educational Practice" indicates how teachers are hamstrung in providing for individual children by limiting factors—expectations for schooling, the institutional curriculum, and school organization. Crutchfield, on creativity, advances three reasons for increased demand for individual instruction, pedagogical, motivational, and social.

Fantini, Mario D., and Gerald Weinstein. *Toward a Contact Curriculum.* New York: Anti-Defamation League of B'nai B'rith (Book Department, 315 Lexington Avenue, New York 10016), 1967.
Attempts to move through a series of curricular approaches from rigid scheduling to flexible scheduling, from symbol-based curriculum to experience-based curriculum, from a horizontally programmed disjoint sequence to a vertical small-step sequence, from a past-and-future orientation to an immediate orientation, from a what curriculum to a why curriculum, from knowing to doing, and from extrinsic content to inner content.

Featherstone, Joseph. *Schools Where Children Learn.* New York: Liveright, 1971.
Reprints from the author's *New Republic* writings comparing English primary school innovations with American elementary school problems. Second part describes specific American school programs designed after the English.

Gagne, Robert M., ed. *Learning and Individual Differences.* A Symposium of the Learning Research and Development Center, University of Pittsburgh. Columbus, Ohio: Charles E. Merrill Books, 1967.
Chapter 2, "How Can Instruction Be Adapted to Individual Differ-

ences?" by Lee Cronbach, and John B. Carroll's discussion which follows are especially pertinent. Other chapters deal with styles of learning and human capabilities related to success in learning different kinds of content.

Gibbons, Maurice. *Individualized Instruction: A Descriptive Analysis.* New York: Teachers College Press, Columbia University, 1971.
An attempt to find some order in the array of programs which are supposed to be "individualized" though few of those programs attend to individual students.

Gleason, Gerald T., ed. *The Theory and Nature of Independent Learning.* Scranton, Pa.: International Textbook Co., 1967.
Six chapters include "Independent Learning" by James Macdonald, "Learning Research and Its Implications" by Robert Gagne, "Implications of Motivation Theory" by Pauline Sears, "A Socio-Anthropological View" by Dorothy Lee, "Technological Developments" by Gerald Gleason, and "A Phenomenological Perspective" by Sidney Jourand.

Goodlad, John I. "Diagnosis and Prescription in Educational Practice." *New Approaches to Individualizing Instruction.* Princeton, New Jersey: Educational Testing Service, 1965, pp. 27–37.
Stresses inductive processes of teaching and learning in a multimedia setting. Role of the teacher becomes partner, data source, observer, and diagnostician.

————. *School, Curriculum, and the Individual.* Waltham, Mass.: Blaisdell Publishing Co., 1966.
Brings together many of Goodlad's writings, including his thinking on instructional decisions which a teacher makes, the learner as a data source for curriculum decisions, and school and classroom organization.

————. *Some Propositions in Search of Schools.* Washington, D.C.: National Education Association, Department of Elementary School Principals, 1962.
Printed version of an address emphasizing need for pupil individuality. Places the nongraded school in perspective of goals of education.

———— and Robert H. Anderson. *The Nongraded Elementary School.* Rev. ed. New York: Harcourt, Brace and World, Inc. 1963.
The definitive work in this area to date. Deals with a wide range of pupil abilities within a classroom, promotion and nonpromotion, the nongraded school in operation, reporting progress in such a school, and the steps in the establishment of nongraded schools. Proposes a curriculum organized vertically around fundamental concepts, principles, and modes of inquiry.

Gordon, Julia. *My Country School Diary: An Adventure in Creative Teaching.* New York: Dell, 1970.
Originally written in the 1930s, the experiences of this creative and

resourceful teacher might very well inspire and add insight to today's teacher who wishes to personalize her teaching.

Great Britain. Central Advisory Council (England). *Children and Their Primary Schools* (Plowden Report). 2 vols. London: Her Majesty's Stationery Office, 1967. Available in U.S. from Sales Section, British Information Services, New York, N.Y. 10022.
Vol. I: The rationale of modern British primary schools, practices, observations, and recommendations. Vol. II: Statistical tables and miscellaneous information.

Gross, Ronald, and Beatrice Gross, eds. *Radical School Reform*. New York: Simon & Schuster, 1969.
Articles by Joseph Featherstone, Jonathan Kozol, John Holt, Paul Goodman, and Edgar Friedenberg.

Hawkins, Frances P. *The Logic of Action: From a Teacher's Notebook*. Boulder, Colo.: Elementary Science Advisory Center, 1969.
Describes work with young deaf children which can be useful to any teacher: "given a rich environment—with open-ended raw materials—children can be encouraged and trusted to take a large part in the design of their own learning."

Heathers, Glen. "Guidelines for Reorganizing School, Classroom, and Curriculum." *Rational Planning in Curriculum and Instruction*. Washington, D.C.: National Education Association, Center for the Study of Instruction, 1967, pp. 63–86.

————. "Individualizing Instruction and Title III, ESEA." *Catalyst for Change: A National Study of ESEA Title III (PACE)*. Notes and Working Papers Concerning the Administration of Programs. Washington, D.C.: U.S. Office of Education, 1967, pp. 177–200.
Examines individualization as provided for in a sample of 43 proposals for Title III projects, and concludes that a majority of them lack "a working understanding of individualized instruction, and of how to plan and conduct programs designed to achieve it." States six recommendations.

Hillson, Maurie, ed. *Change and Innovation in Elementary School Organization: Selected Readings*. New York: Holt, Rinehart and Winston, Inc., 1965.
Selected readings concerning the current popular ideas for elementary school reorganization. Included are articles on ability or partial-ability grouping plans; departmentalization and limited-departmentalization plans; team teaching and coordinate and collaborative teaching; the dual progress plan, multi-grade and multi-age grouping; and nongraded movement in the elementary school.

Holt, John. *How Children Fail*. New York: Dell Publishing Company, Inc., 1965.
A personal, intuitive, subjective documentary of a teacher who watches children being taught and decides "they fail to develop

more than a tiny part of the tremendous capacity for learning, understanding, and creating with which they are born." Holt suggests schools in which each child can satisfy his curiosity in his own way, develop his talents, pursue his interests, and gain from his teachers an idea of the excitement and richness of life.

————. *How Children Learn.* New York: Pitman Publishing Corp., 1967. Illustrates the spontaneous ways in which children embrace knowledge before they enter schools where they "learn to be stupid." Holt's system: A teacher's role is to "give children as much help and guidance as they need and ask for, listen respectfully when they feel like talking, and then get out of their way."

————. *What Do I Do Monday?* New York: E. P. Dutton & Co., 1970. Brings up to date Holt's theories of education based on the idea of learning as a growth process best nourished by openness and freedom. Adds a how-to-do-it section, with practical classroom examples from the fields of mathematics, reading, and writing.

Howes, Virgil M., et al. *Individualization of Instruction: Exploring Open-Structure.* Los Angeles, Calif.: Educational Inquiry, Inc. (ASUCLA Student Store, 308 Westwood Plaza, Los Angeles 90024), 1968. Helen Darrow, Louise Tyler, Robert Keuscher, and Virgil Howes probe in depth one model of individualized instruction—the open-structure learning environment. Focuses on self-direction, self-responsibility, and learner autonomy in the schooling phase of education.

————. *Individualization of Instruction: A Search.* Los Angeles, Calif.: Educational Inquiry, Inc. (ASUCLA Student Store, 308 Westwood Plaza, Los Angeles 90024), 1967. Chapter 1, "Why Individualize Instruction?" by Robert Keuscher; Chapter 2, "Individualization As a Process and a Method," by Madeline Hunter; Chapter 3, "Modes of Individualizing Instruction," by Virgil Howes; Chapter 4, "Models of Individualized Instruction," by Louise Tyler.

————. *Individualization of Instruction: A Teaching Strategy.* New York: The Macmillan Company, 1970. Readings attack the questions: Why individualize? What is individualization? What programs and practices are helpful? Contributors include Virgil Howes, Robert Keuscher, Madeline Hunter, Bernice Wolfson, Jeanette Veatch, Dwight Allen, Paul Goodman, Robert Glaser, and Joseph Featherstone.

Howson, Geoffrey, ed. *Children at School: Primary Education in Britain Today.* Published for the Center for Curriculum Renewal and Educational Development Overseas (CREDO). London: Heinemann, 1969. Available in the United States from Teachers College, Columbia University, New York. British primary education since the Plowden Report, written by experts in the field.

Hunter, Madeline. *Motivation Theory for Teachers.* El Segundo, Calif.: TIP Publications (P.O. Box 514, El Segundo 90245), 1967.

————. *Reinforcement Theory for Teachers.* El Segundo, Calif.: TIP Publications (P.O. Box 514, El Segundo 90245), 1967.

————. *Retention Theory for Teachers.* El Segundo, Calif.: TIP Publications (P.O. Box 514, El Segundo 90245), 1967.
Programmed texts on the application of psychological research in the fields of motivation, reinforcement, and retention theory, translated into a form usable by classroom teachers in the daily teaching act.

Individualized Instruction Association. *Individualized Instruction and the Grouping of Pupils.* Sixth Annual Conference hosted by California Western University in cooperation with the Department of Education, San Diego County. Pasco, Washington: R. Wallace Pischel, Inc., 1967.
Major speeches: John I. Goodlad, "Perspective on Individualized Instruction"; Newton Metfessel, "Psychological Perspectives on Individualized Instruction"; Jimmy E. Nations, "Individualization: A Realistic Approach"; and W. Ballentine Henley, "Individualization, Excellence and Achievement." Notes on section meetings dealing with various phases of individual instruction.

Informal Schools in Britain Today. 23 vols. New York: Citation Press, 1971.
This paperback series is a joint venture of the Ford Foundation and the Schools Council of England. Includes: *The Pupil's Day; The Teacher's Role; An Infant School; The Headteacher's Role; The Government of Education; From Home to School; Space, Time and Grouping; A Junior School; A Rural School; Towards Informality;* and *An Introduction* by Joseph Featherstone.

Institute for Development of Educational Activities, Inc. *The British Infant School.* Melbourne, Fla.: the Institute, 1969.
Report of an international seminar examining the developments in the infant schools of Britain with position statements by Lady Plowden and Miss E. Marianne Parry. Identifies exemplary practices which might well be useful in the United States. A companion film to this report, *The British Infant School,* is listed in Part IV.

————. *The Open Classroom: Informal Education in America.* Dayton, Ohio: the Institute, 1972.
Discusses the advantages and possible pitfalls in initiating and operating an informal classroom. The teacher's role, appropriate environment, and activities are treated and graphically illustrated.

————. *Tell Us What To Do! But—Don't Tell Me What To Do!* Melbourne, Fla.: the Institute, 1971.
Comments and articles from teachers in the League of Cooperating Schools involved in the |I|D|E|A| five-year Study of Educational

Change and School Improvement. Individualization of instruction was a major effort on the part of some of these teachers.

Kagan, Jerome, ed. *Creativity and Learning*. Boston, Mass.: Beacon Press, 1968.
Readings stress the encouragement of heterogeneity, even at the cost of efficiency: Philip Jackson and Samuel Messick, "The Person, the Product, and the Response"; Donald Mackinnon, "The Study of Creative Persons"; Michael Wallach, "Creativity and the Expression of Possibilities"; Jerome Kagan, "Personality and the Learning Process"; and David Hawkins, "The Informed Vision."

Kohl, Herbert R. *The Open Classroom*. New York: Vintage Books, 1970.
Brief paperback offers practical help to teachers who wish to try a new way of teaching but stay within the public school system.

Kozol, Jonathan. *Free Schools*. Boston: Houghton Mifflin, 1972.
Believes education should be individualized, open-structured, and unoppressive but insists that teachers *can* teach reading and should because some need it to survive in the present system. "There has to be a way to find pragmatic competence, internal peace, and ethical passion all in the same process."

Lee, Dorris M. *Diagnostic Teaching*. Washington, D.C.: National Education Association, Department of Elementary-Kindergarten-Nursery Education, 1966.
A pamphlet which emphasizes the uniqueness of each child, takes exception to practices ignoring this, and promotes the idea of self-directed learning. Offers suggestions for implementing these beliefs in various curriculum areas.

Leonard, George. *Education and Ecstasy*. New York: Delacorte Press, 1968.
A startling book—explores the capabilities of the human organism, the limitations and enhancement capabilities of the outer environment in development of man, and the interaction between environment and the organism. "The Rogue As Teacher," a fascinating chapter on divergent teachers, is followed by an imaginary flight into future education. Controversial, to say the least.

Lindvall, C. Mauritz, and John O. Bolvin. *Individually Prescribed Instruction: The Oakleaf Project*. Working Paper 8. Pittsburgh: University of Pittsburgh, Learning Research and Development Center, 1966.
Describes a program in which the major goal is to permit pupils to proceed through a sequential set of objectives for a given subject at a pace determined by individual ability and interest.

Lippitt, Ronald, Robert Fox, et al. *Understanding Classroom Social Relations and Learning*. Chicago: Science Research Associates (259 E. Erie St., Chicago 60611), 1966.
Examines the theories and research findings on which three useful booklets are based: *Problem Solving to Improve Classroom Learn-*

ing, Diagnosing Classroom Learning Environments, and *Role-Playing Methods in the Classroom.*

Macdonald, James B. "The Person in the Curriculum." *Precedents and Promise in the Curriculum Field,* edited by Helen F. Robison. New York: Teachers College Press, 1966, pp. 38–52.

————, Bernice J. Wolfson, and Esther Zaret. *Reschooling Society: A Conceptual Model.* Washington, D.C.: Association for Supervision and Curriculum Development, 1973.
Provides a much needed theoretical base for person-oriented schools by restructuring the sociocultural, psychological, and transactional dimensions of schooling into a rational whole.

Marsh, Leonard. *Alongside the Child: Experiences in the English Primary School.* New York: Praeger Publishing Co., 1970.
A literate description of the best practices in primary education. Treats various subject areas.

Moustakas, Clark. *The Authentic Teacher: Sensitivity and Awareness in the Classroom.* Cambridge, Mass.: Howard A. Doyle Publishing Co., 1966.
Promotes the dignity of the child, openness by the teacher, honesty in interpersonal encounters. Freedom, the capacity to choose, and responsibility are stressed.

Murrow, Casey, and Liza Murrow. *Children Come First: The Inspired Work of English Primary Schools.* New York: American Heritage Press, 1971.
These two inspired authors describe their year of intensive study of the English schools providing insights, specifics, and many practical suggestions including the use of restraint when attempting to emulate them.

National Association for the Education of Young Children. *Open Education: The Legacy of the Progressive Movement,* edited by Georgianna Engstrom. Washington, D.C.: the Association, 1970.
A conference report including papers by David Elkind, James Macdonald, Roma Gans, Vincent Rogers, and Bernard Spodek.

National Education Association, Project on the Instruction Program of the Public School. *Planning and Organizing for Teaching* by John I. Goodlad (one of the major reports of the project). Washington, D.C.: the Association, 1963.
Data on "individual differences" permeate this entire volume, but pp. 9–16 set down guiding values and propositions about learners which are particularly helpful. "Inter-individual differences" are delineated as distinct from "intra-individual differences." Chapter 3 discusses a model for learner-centered, nongraded school organization.

National Society for the Study of Education. *The Changing American School.* 65th Yearbook, Part II, edited by John I. Goodlad. Chicago: University of Chicago Press, 1966.

Describes and analyzes selected educational changes, relating such changes to societal forces of the past decade. Goodlad authors Chapter 2, "The Curriculum." Chapter 5, "School Organization," by Glen Heathers, examines nongrading and team teaching as examples of change. Instructional resources, the teacher, and the schoolhouse in transition are also treated.

————. *Individualizing Instruction*. 61st Yearbook, Part I, edited by Nelson B. Henry. Chicago: University of Chicago Press, 1962.

This definitive work offers a comprehensive look at what individualized instruction entails. Discusses "Conditions tending to encourage or suppress individual differences," such as biology, society, the school, the curriculum, and the teacher. Gives illustrations of individual differences at various age levels and current school practices for individualizing instruction. John I. Goodlad has a helpful chapter on individual differences and vertical organization of the school.

Neill, A. S. *Freedom—Not License!* New York: Hart Publishing Co., Inc., 1966.

Further explanation of the philosophy set forth in *Summerhill*—every child is entitled to freedom, an excess of freedom constitutes license. Explains how and where the line is drawn between these two in anti-life attitudes, school, sex, childhood, adolescence, and adulthood.

Nuffield Foundation. *I Do, and I Understand*. New York: John Wiley & Sons, 1967.

Presents a contemporary approach to mathematics for children from five to thirteen stressing "how to learn" not "what to teach." This guide faces the problems brought in by a new approach and attempts to show how they can be overcome.

Parker, Don H. *Schooling for Individual Excellence*. Camden, N.J.: Thomas Nelson & Sons, 1963.

Chapters 16 through 20 deal with the problems of providing instruction suitable for children who differ widely in performance levels. Helpful bibliography is included.

Peck, Robert F. *Promoting Self-Disciplined Learning: A Researchable Revolution*. Washington, D.C.: U.S. Office of Education, 1970.

An experimental program now underway in Austin, Texas, is aimed at meeting some of these research needs: 1) to train teachers in the use of individualized instruction methods, 2) research on the effects of such training, and 3) research on the differential effects of particular teachers on particular kinds of students. In a continuing cycle, the teacher tailors her treatment of the child to his specific situation, observes whether the tactic works or not, then discusses it with consultants and revises it.

Peters, R. S., ed. *Perspectives on Plowden*. London: Routledge & Kegan Paul, 1969.

The faculty of London University's Institute of Education takes a critical stance toward the child-centered primary school as described in the Plowden Report.

Plowden, Lady Bridget (see Great Britain. Central Advisory Council [England]. *Children and Their Primary Schools* [Plowden Report]).

Postman, Neil, and Charles Weingartner. *Teaching As a Subversive Activity.* New York: Delacorte Press, 1969.

A highly critical attack on traditional teaching and school organization. Suggests an inductive approach to learning emphasizing problem-solving. Authors give detailed example in the area of Language Arts (English) to show it can be done.

Rathbone, Charles H., ed. *Open Education: The Informal Classroom.* New York: Citation Press, 1971.

John Holt introduces this selection of articles on open education. Includes William Hull's "Leicestershire Revisted," Tony Kallet's "Two Classrooms," and Allan Leitman and Edith Churchill's "Approximation No. 1" on the physical environment.

Research for Better Schools, Inc. *A Progress Report: Individually Prescribed Instruction.* Philadelphia: the Corporation, 1969.

Illustrated booklet describing background and program of the Learning Research and Development Center at Pittsburgh, types of diagnostic instruments used, and evaluation process. Answers general questions about IPI.

Richardson, Elwyn S. *In the Early World.* Wellington, N.Z.: New Zealand Council of Educational Research (22 Brandon St., Wellington, N.Z.), 1964.

Records an eight-year experiment in Oruaiti, New Zealand, where each classroom was allowed to "uniquely express its own mode of co-operative individualism." Many illustrations of children's work.

Rogers, Carl. *Freedom to Learn.* Columbus, Ohio: Charles E. Merrill, 1969.

Rogers' first book addressed directly to educators, collecting the ideas scattered through his writings on the interpersonal learning relationship. Describes applications at various levels including his own at the graduate level of education.

————. "Learning To Be Free." In *Conflict and Creativity: Control of the Mind,* by F. M. Barber and R. H. Wilson. New York: McGraw-Hill Book Co., 1963, pp. 268–288.

Rogers, Vincent. *Teaching in the British Primary School.* New York: Macmillan, 1970.

A selection of papers, some in specific curriculum areas, contributed mostly by experienced British educators. See also his article in *Phi Delta Kappan,* v. 51, October 1969, "English and American Primary Schools." Rogers considers the purposes underlying the program of education of utmost significance.

Russell, James E. *Change and Challenge in American Education*. Boston: Houghton Mifflin Co., 1965.
Sees the shift in the philosophical and social context of the twentieth century as a challenge to educators which requires them to make new responses. The response in elementary education, as the author sees it, is of utmost importance since he feels "the elementary school has the most intense impact of any school in our educational system." It can establish effective contact with each child, give individual attention, seek greater intellectual resources for individual study, motivate its pupils to learn, and develop the child's ability to think.

Sargent, Betsye. *The Integrated Day in an American School*. Boston, Mass.: National Association of Independent Schools, 1970.
Full notes on a year's teaching at the Shady Hill School in Cambridge, Massachusetts, offering specific lesson plans, activities, materials, and learning space arrangements.

Silberman, Charles E. *Crisis in the Classroom*. New York: Random House, 1970.
Reports a three-year investigation of American public education commissioned by the Carnegie Corporation in which the author reviews much ground covered by other critics such as Paul Goodman, Kenneth Clark, James Conant, and Herbert Kohl. He finds, in agreement, most schools are "grim" and "joyless" places. Especially informative on individualized programs. There are chapters on the schools of North Dakota.

Silberman, Melvin, et al., eds. *The Psychology of Open Teaching and Learning: An Inquiry Approach*. Boston: Little, Brown and Company, 1972.
Readings selected to demonstrate the value of student-directed inquiry for learning. Well-known authorities write on the learning environment, cognitive functioning, and the teaching process.

Sutton, Audrey. *Ordered Freedom*. Encino, Calif.: International Center for Educational Development, 1970.
Head of Stebon Primary School describes the freer, more informal, more child-centered situation found in many British primary schools. How the school became that way, the guiding philosophy, what the teachers did, and what happened in the school setting as well as specifics in subject areas are reported.

Thelen, Herbert A., et al. *Classroom Grouping for Teachability*. New York: John Wiley & Sons, 1967.
"How can the resources of teachers and students be utilized more effectively for educational purposes in the classroom?" The rationale, procedure, and results of a three-year research investigation of this question are reported here. Stresses the value of student–teacher communication and compatibility grouping.

Thomas, R. Murray, and Shirley M. Thomas. *Individual Differences in the Classroom.* New York: David McKay Co., 1965.
Focuses on intellectual differences, differences in specialized abilities, and psychophysical differences. Treats these aspects of students' personalities in a practical manner, offering suggestions to teachers about specific methods, materials, and classroom organization.

Torrance, E. Paul, and R. D. Strom, eds. *Mental Health and Achievement.* New York: John Wiley & Sons, 1965.
Responses of more than thirty authors requested to address themselves to topics concerning personal development. Torrance's chapter, "Different Ways of Learning for Different Kinds of Children," will assist school personnel, parents, and community leaders in the improvement of their roles.

Vermont State Department of Education. *Vermont Design of Education.* Montpelier: State Department of Education, 1968.
Seventeen premises "constitute a goal, an ideal, a student-centered philosophy for the process of education in Vermont."

Wallach, Michael A., and Nathan Kogan. *Modes of Thinking in Young Children.* New York: Holt, Rinehart and Winston, Inc., 1965.
A careful study showing that creativity is independent of general intelligence. It advances our understanding of differences among children as they affect behavior in the school environment. Categorizing and conceptualization, sensitivity to physiognomic properties, and the role of anxiety and defensiveness are examined closely as the variables relating to intelligence and creativity jointly. Concludes with implications for education, proposing cognitive enterprises free from connections with the stress of academic evaluation such as grades and competitive procedures.

Washburne, Carleton W., and Sidney P. Marland, Jr. *Winnetka: The History and Significance of an Educational Experiment.* Englewood Cliffs, N.J.: Prentice-Hall, 1963.
Describes individualized self-instruction in Winnetka, Illinois, schools of forty years ago: an educational plan calling for construction of instructional materials that the child could handle without direct intervention of teachers and with self-evaluation and collective responsibility.

Weber, Lillian. *The English Infant School and Informal Education.* Englewood Cliffs, N.J.: Prentice-Hall, 1971.
A careful account based on close observation of schools for young children in England using the informal classroom.

Wees, Wilfred R. *Nobody Can Teach Anyone Anything.* Garden City, N.Y.: Doubleday & Co., Inc., 1971.
Raises questions about our current practice, suggesting that it is up to us to change ourselves and our practices, not the child, who learns on his own.

Williams, Lois E. *Independent Learning in the Elementary School Classroom*. Washington, D.C.: National Education Association, American Association of Elementary-Kindergarten-Nursery Educators, 1969.
A practical pamphlet guide to teachers in setting up learning centers, organizing free-activity periods, helping children make choices, and checking on their growth.

Wolfson, Bernice J. *Moving Toward Personalized Learning and Teaching*. Encino, Calif.: International Center for Educational Development, 1969.
A collection of articles and speeches by an experienced educator in the field of individualization of instruction.

Yeomans, Edward. *Education for Initiative and Responsibility*. Boston: National Association of Independent Schools (4 Liberty Square, Boston 02109), 1967.
Describes the "integrated day," an outgrowth of the Leicestershire, England, infant schools (children of five to seven). Records a day's events and a visitor's reflections. Discusses vertical grouping and necessary equipment. A break from tradition demonstrating a provocative strategy for educational communities.

————. *The Wellsprings of Teaching*. Boston, Mass.: National Association of Independent Schools, 1969.
A report of a teachers' workshop on the philosophy and techniques of the integrated day. "Integrated day" is defined as a controlled but responsive environment, free from traditional authorities and conformities, containing materials, books, or people which induce learning experiences among children in which the teacher can exert selection and control of the environment to see that these experiences are educational. Children choose how they wish to spend their time, relying less on the teacher and more on resources available and thus become relatively independent learners.

Young, Milton A. *Teaching Children with Special Learning Needs: A Problem Solving Approach*. New York: John Day Co., 1967.
Chapter 3, "Individual Evaluation: The Key to Effective Planning," presents the practical aspects of evaluation with guidelines, suggestions, and instruments. Chapter 6 suggests activities and practices for overcoming individual or group learning problems.

Younie, William J. *Instructional Approaches to Slow Learning*. New York: Bureau of Publications, Teachers College Press, Columbia University, 1967.
Practical help in connection with a wide range of subject matter areas covering the elementary and secondary levels. Discusses the approaches of educational innovations. Two appendices contain annotated lists of teaching materials for use with slow learners and a basic reference library for teachers.

Magazine Articles and Periodicals

Allen, Dwight W. "Individualized Instruction." *CTA Journal,* 61: 27, 43–50, October 1965.

Barth, Roland S. "So You Want To Change to an Open Classroom." *Phi Delta Kappan,* 53: 97–99, October 1971.

Bloom, Benjamin S. "Learning for Mastery." *UCLA Evaluation Comment,* May 1968.

Bradley, Philip A. "Individualized Instruction through Cooperative Teaching and a Programmed Text." *National Elementary Principal,* 43: 46–49, May 1964.

Bremer, John. "A Curriculum, a Vigor, a Local Abstraction . . ." *The Center Forum,* 3: 1, 4–5, March 1, 1969.

Brenner, Anton. "Re-examining Readiness." *Childhood Education,* 43: 453–457, April 1967.

Brown, B. Frank. "A New Design for Individual Learning." *Journal of Secondary Education,* 37: 368–375, October 1962.

California Journal for Instructional Improvement. 14: 2, May 1971.
A special section on Open Education includes: Virgil M. Howes, "Making School a Way of Life"; Robert Keuscher, "Individualization of Instruction: What It Is and What It Isn't"; Howes, "Patterns for Pupil Decision-Making and Planning"; Howes and Keuscher, "Building the Learning Environment"; Douglas Dale, "A Change of Attitude"; and Carrie Haynes, "A Happening in a Ghetto School."

Combs, Arthur W. "Fostering Self-Direction." *Educational Leadership,* 23: 373–376, February 1966.

Cook, Ann, and Herbert Mack. "The British Primary School." *Educational Leadership,* 27: 140–143, November 1969.

Danowski, Charles E. "Individualization of Instruction: A Functional Definition." *IAR-Research Bulletin,* 5: 1–5, February 1965.

Doll, Ronald C. "Fostering Student Individuality in the Schools." *Education Digest,* 30: 8–11, May 1965.

Drummond, T. Darrell. "Freedom To Grow." *Childhood Education,* 43: 26–28, September 1966.

Dugger, Chester W. "A Teacher Discovers Individualized Instruction." *Elementary School Journal,* 71: 357–360, April 1971.

Durrell, Donald D., et al. "Adapting Instruction to the Learning Needs of Children in the Intermediate Grades." *Journal of Education,* 142: 1–78, December 1959.

Featherstone, Joseph. "Report Analysis: Children and Their Primary Schools." *Harvard Educational Review,* 38: 317–328, Spring 1968.
Describes American attempts to introduce the practices of open education as suggested in the Plowden Report. Stresses the importance of building a climate conducive to educational change.

————. "How Children Learn." *New Republic,* 157: 17–21, September 2, 1967.

————. "Schools for Children." *New Republic,* 157: 17–21, August 19, 1967.

————. "Teaching Children To Think." *New Republic,* 157: 15–19, September 9, 1967.

Fischer, Barbara B., and Louis Fischer. "Toward Individualized Learning." *The Elementary School Journal,* 69: 298–303, March 1969.

Glatthorn, Allan A., and J. E. Ferderbar. "Independent Study—For All Students." *Phi Delta Kappan,* 47: 379–382, March 1966.

Goodlad, John I. "Nongraded Schools: Meeting Children Where They Are." *Saturday Review,* 48: 57–59, 72–74, March 20, 1965.

Gross, Beatrice, and Ronald Gross. "A Little Bit of Chaos." *Saturday Review,* 53: 71–73, May 16, 1970.

Hapgood, Marilyn. "The Open Classroom, Protect It from Its Friends." *Saturday Review,* 54: 66–69, 75, September 18, 1971.

Hart, Leslie A. "Learning at Random." *Saturday Review,* 52: 62–63, April 19, 1969.

Hawkins, David. "Childhood and the Education of Intellectuals." *Harvard Educational Review,* 36: 477–483, Fall 1966.

Heaps, Kathleen. "Setting Up an Integrated Day in an Infants' School." *Froebel Journal,* 17: 11–21, June 1970.
A practicing teacher tells of the gradual transition from a formal school timetable to a flexible unstructured day.

Herbst, Jurgen. "The Anti-School—Some Reflections on Teaching." *Educational Theory,* 18: 13–22, Winter 1966.

Herrick, Virgil E. "Curriculum Decisions and Provision for Individual Differences." *Elementary School Journal,* 62: 313–320, March 1962.

"Human Variability: The Insistent Element." *Educational Leadership,* 24: March 1967, entire issue.

Hunter, Madeline C. "Individualized Instruction." *Instructor,* 53–63, March 1970.

————. "When the Teacher Diagnoses Learning." *Educational Leadership,* 23: 545–549, April 1966.

————. "The Dimensions of Nongrading." *Elementary School Journal,* 65: 20–25, October 1964.

———— and M. G. Wagner. "The Case Conference." *Elementary School Journal,* 67: 303–309, March 1967.

Jackson, John W. "The Individualized School." *Journal of Secondary Education,* 41: 195–200, May 1966.

Jasik, Marilyn. "Breaking Barriers by Individualizing." *Childhood Education,* 45: 65–74, October 1968.
Seven brief anecdotes from classroom teachers report individual ways to "penetrate the learning blockade."

Lonsway, Francis A. "Focus on the Individual in School Administration." *NASSP Bulletin,* 49: 80–86, September 1965.

Miel, Alice. "Sequence in Learning." *Education Digest,* 32: 35–38, April 1967.

Mukerjii, Rose. "Roots in Early Childhood for Continuous Learning." *Childhood Education,* 42: 28–34, September 1965.

Nyquist, Ewald B. "The Concept of Open Education: Its Philosophy, Historical Perspectives, and Implications." *Education Digest,* 9–12, November 1971.
Also in *Science Teacher,* 38: 25–28, September 1971.

Parker, Don H. "When Should I Individualize Instruction?" *Grade Teacher,* 79: 66–67, 136–37, April 1962.

Rasmussen, Glen R. "Our Common Neglect of Individual Differences." *The Clearing House,* 37: 3–7, September 1962.

Rathbone, Charles H. "A Lesson from Loughborough." *This Magazine Is About Schools,* 3: 121–127, Winter 1969.

Spaulding, Robert L. "Personalized Education in Southside School," *Elementary School Journal,* 70: 180–189, January 1970.

Thelen, Herbert A. "Pupil Self-Direction." *NASSP Bulletin,* 50: 99–109, April 1966.

Tomkins, Ellsworth. "Individual Differences in the 1960's—Their Implications for School Administrators." *NASSP Bulletin,* 46: 1–7, April 1962.

"Toward New Goals for Individualization." *Educational Leadership,* 29:4, January 1972.
Articles deal with emerging definitions, problems, and programs in individualizing instruction.

"Toward Self-Direction," *Educational Leadership,* 23:5, February 1966.

Tway, Eileen. "A Self-Feeding Schedule for Children in Elementary School." *Childhood Education,* 69: 68–71, November 1968.
Self-contained third grade classroom using large blocks of time for self-selected activities.

Ulin, Donald S. "What I Learned from the British Schools." *Grade Teacher,* 86: February 1969.

Veatch, Jeannette. "Improving Independent Study." *Childhood Education,* 43: 284–288, January 1967.

Walberg, Herbert J. "Optimizing and Individualizing Instruction: Some Traditions, Domains, and Models." *Interchange,* 2: 15–27, 1971.

———— and Susan C. Thomas. "Open Education: An Operational Definition and Validation in Great Britain and United States." *American Educational Research Journal,* 9: 197–207, Spring 1972.

Wolfson, Bernice J. "Individualization of Instruction." *Journal of the Reading Specialist,* 5: 45–53, December 1965.

———. "Individualizing Instruction." *NEA Journal,* 55: 31–35, November 1966.

———. "Pupil and Teacher Roles in Individualized Instruction." *The Elementary School Journal,* 68: 357–366, April 1968.

———. "The Promise of Multiage Grouping for Individualizing Instruction." *Elementary School Journal,* 67: 354–362, April 1967.

——— and Shirlyn Nash. "Perceptions of Decision-Making in Elementary School Classrooms." *Elementary School Journal,* 69: 89 ff., November 1968.

Pertinent Periodicals

Big Rock Candy Mountain. Menlo Park, California: Portola Institute. Six-year-old educational offshoot of *Whole Earth Catalog* reviews great variety of educational materials.

Insights (Newsletter). University of North Dakota, New School of Behavioral Studies in Education, Grand Forks, North Dakota 58201.

Learning: The Magazine for Creative Teaching. Boulder, Colo.: 1255 Portland Place, Boulder, Colorado 80302.
Published nine times a year, during school year.

Manas. Los Angeles, California: Manas Publishing Co., P.O. Box 32112, El Sereno Station, Los Angeles.
Fortnightly. Section on "Children and Ourselves."

New Schools Exchange Newsletter. Santa Barbara, California: 2840 Hidden Valley Lane, Santa Barbara, California 93103.
Fortnightly. Describes experimental and free schools and their personnel.

Outlook. Boulder, Colorado: Mountain View Center for Environmental Education, University of Colorado 80302.
New periodical on how children think, classroom arrangements, teaching materials and ideas.

This Magazine Is About Schools. P.O. Box 876, Terminal "A," Toronto 1, Ontario, Canada.
Quarterly. Radical in approach and substance.

PART II: SUBJECT AREAS
Reading
Books and Pamphlets

Barbe, Walter B. *Educators' Guide to Personalized Reading Instruction.* Englewood Cliffs, N.J.: Prentice-Hall, 1961.

Brogan, Peggy, and L. K. Fox. *Helping Children Read.* New York: Holt, Rinehart and Winston, Inc., 1961.

Claremont Unified School District. *The Sycamore Instructional Program: A Non-graded Team Approach.* Claremont, Calif.: the District, 1967.

Darrow, Helen F., and Virgil M. Howes. *Approaches to Individualized Reading.* New York: Appleton-Century-Crofts, 1960.

Fader, Daniel. *The Naked Children.* New York: Macmillan, 1971.

Frazier, A. "Individualized Reading Program." *Conference on Reading.* Chicago: University of Chicago Press, 1961, pp. 57–74.

Howes, Virgil M. *Individualizing Instruction in Reading and Social Studies: Selected Readings on Programs and Practices.* New York: The Macmillan Company, 1970.

Lazar, May. *A Practical Guide to Individualized Reading.* Publication 40. Brooklyn: Bureau of Educational Research, New York Board of Education, 1960.

Lee, Dorris M., and R. V. Allen. *Learning to Read Through Experience.* 2nd ed. New York: Appleton-Century-Crofts, 1965.

Miel, Alice. *Individualizing Reading Practices.* New York: Bureau of Publications, Teachers College Press, Columbia University, 1958.

Nielsen, Wilhelmina. "Twenty Language Experiences Which Form the Framework of the Experience Approach to the Language Arts." *Claremont College Reading Conference.* Twenty-ninth Yearbook. Claremont, Calif.: Claremont Graduate School and University Center, 1965, pp. 168–174.

Povey, Gail, and Jeanne Fryer. *Personalized Reading: A Chance for Everyone.* Encino, Calif.: International Center for Educational Development, 1972.

Ramsey, Wallace Z., ed. *Organizing for Individual Differences.* Newark, Del.: International Reading Association (Box 695, Newark 19711), 1967 (Perspectives in Reading No. 9).

Strang, Ruth. "Effective Use of Classroom Organization in Meeting Individual Differences." *Meeting Individual Differences in Reading,* ed. by H. Alan Robinson. Chicago: University of Chicago Press, 1964, pp. 164–170.

Veatch, Jeannette. *Individualizing Your Reading Program.* New York: G. P. Putnam's Sons, 1959.

———— with Philip J. Acinapuro. *Reading in the Elementary School.* New York: Ronald Press Co., 1966.

Magazine Articles

Balow, Irving H. "Does Homogeneous Grouping Give Homogeneous Groups?" *Elementary School Journal,* 63: 28–32, October 1962.

Duker, Sam. "Needed Research on Individualized Reading." *Elementary English,* 43: 220–225, 246, March 1966.

Frazier, Alexander. "Individualized Reading: More Than New Forms and Formulas." *Elementary English,* 39: 809–814, December 1962.

Groff, Patrick J. "Helping Teachers Begin Individualized Reading." *National Elementary Principal,* 43: 47–50, February 1964.

Robinson, Helen M. "Individualized Reading." *Elementary School Journal,* 60: 411–420, May 1960.

Smith, Nila B. "Individualized Instruction: Concepts Old and New." *Education,* 81: 527–529, May 1961.

———. "Something Old, Something New in Primary Reading." *Elementary English,* 37: 368–374, October 1964.

Spencer, Doris U. "Individualized First Grade Reading Versus a Basal Reader Program in Rural Communities." *Reading Teacher,* 19: 595–600, May 1966.

Veatch, Jeannette. "In Defense of Individualized Reading." *Elementary English,* 37: 227–233, April 1960.

———. "Structure in the Reading Program." *Elementary English,* 44: 252–256, March 1967.

Witty, Paul A. "Individualized Reading: A Postscript." *Elementary English,* 41: 211–217, March 1964.

Language Arts

Books and Pamphlets

Applegate, Mauree. *Easy in English.* Evanston, Ill.: Row, Peterson & Company, 1960.

Burrows, Alvina T. *Teaching Children in the Middle Grades.* Boston, Mass.: D. C. Heath & Company, 1952.

———, et al. *They All Want to Write.* Rev. ed. New York: Prentice-Hall, 1952.

Clegg, Alec B., ed. *The Excitement of Writing.* London: Chatto & Windus, Ltd., 1964.

Moffett, James. *A Student-Centered Language Arts Curriculum, Grades K–6: A Handbook for Teachers.* Boston: Houghton Mifflin Co., 1968.

Magazine Articles

Arnold, F. "Individualized Reading and the Language Arts." *Elementary English,* 39: 269–273, March 1962.

Bergman, F. L. "Individualization: Key to More Writing." *English Journal,* 51: 192–196, March 1962.

Edgerton, Alice K., and R. W. Twombly. "A Programmed Course in Spelling." *Elementary School Journal,* 62: 380–386, April 1962.

Eisenhardt, Cathryn T. "Individualization of Instruction." *Elementary English,* 48: 341–345, March 1971.

Eisman, Edward. "Individualizing Spelling." *Elementary English,* 39: 478–480, May 1962; 40: 529–530, May 1963.

Gilstrap, Robert. "The Development of Independent Spelling Skills in the Intermediate Grades." *Elementary English,* 39: 481–483, May 1962.

Hall, Norman. "Individualize Your Spelling Instruction." *Elementary English,* 39: 476–477, May 1962.

Ham, Jane F. "Success Story: Individualized Spelling." *Instructor,* 75: 145, 171, September 1965.

Mersand, Joseph. "Individualizing Instruction in English in Large and Small Classes." *NASSP Bulletin,* 44: 111–123, March 1960.

Potter, Lois S. "A Plan for Individualized Speech Activities in the Elementary School." *Speech Teacher,* 15: 200–206, September 1966.

Mathematics

Books and Pamphlets

Biggs, Edith E., et al. *Freedom to Learn.* Menlo Park, Calif.: Addison-Wesley, 1969.

Howes, Virgil M. *Individualizing Instruction in Science and Mathematics: Selected Readings on Programs, Practices, and Uses of Technology.* New York: The Macmillan Co., 1970.
Joseph Lipson, Raymond O'Toole, Fred Weaver, Lola May, John Matthews and Charlotte Ryan, Rose Grossman, Patrick Suppes, Anthony Oettinger, David Stansfield, and Norman Kurland are among the contributors.

Nuffield Foundation. *Nuffield Mathematics Project: Computation and Structure, Beginnings, Pictorial Representation, Mathematics Begins; I Do and I Understand.* New York: John Wiley & Sons, 1967.
Teacher's Guides, Weaving Guides, and Check-up Guides.

Sawyer, W. W. *A Path to Modern Mathematics.* New York: Penguin, 1966.

Schools Council for the Curriculum and Examinations. *Mathematics in Primary Schools: Curriculum Bulletin No. 1.* 2nd ed. London: Her Majesty's Stationery Office, 1966. Available in the U.S. through Sales Section, British Information Services, New York, N.Y. 10022.
Reports work done by master teachers who sparked the math revolution in Britain.

Magazine Articles

Biggs, Edith E. "Math Labs and Teachers' Centers—The Math Revolution in Britain." *The Arithmetic Teacher,* 15: 400–408, May 1968.

Flournoy, Frances. "Meeting Individual Differences in Arithmetic." *Arithmetic Teacher,* 7: 80–86, February 1960.

Graham, William A. "Individualized Teaching of Fifth- and Sixth-Grade Arithmetic." *Arithmetic Teacher,* 11: 233–234, April 1964.

Grossman, Rose. "Problem-Solving Observed in British Primary Schools." *The Arithmetic Teacher,* 15: 34–38, January 1969.

Hudgins, Bryce G. "Effects of Group Experience on Individual Problem Solving." *Journal of Educational Psychology,* 51: 37–42, January 1960.

Keffer, Eugene R. "Individualizing Arithmetic Teaching." *Arithmetic Teacher,* 8: 248–250, May 1961.

May, Lola. "Individualized Instruction in a Learning Laboratory Setting." *Arithmetic Teacher,* 13: 110–112, February 1966.

Moench, Laurel. "Individualized Practice in Arithmetic." *Arithmetic Teacher,* 9: 321–329, October 1962.

Moser, Harold E. "Levels of Learning (Planning in Depth)." *Arithmetic Teacher,* 3: 221–225, December 1956.

Potamkin, Caroline S. "An Experiment in Individualized Arithmetic." *Elementary School Journal,* 64: 155–162, December 1963.

Redbird, Helen. "Individualizing Arithmetic Instruction." *Arithmetic Teacher,* 11: 348–349, May 1964.

Searight, Franklin. "You Can Individualize Arithmetic Instruction." *Arithmetic Teacher,* 11: 199–200, March 1964.

Weaver, J. Fred. "Differentiated Instruction and School-Class Organization for Mathematical Learning Within the Elementary Grades." *Arithmetic Teacher,* 13: 495–506, October 1966.

Whitaker, Walter L. "Individualized Arithmetic—An Idea to Improve the Traditional Program." *Arithmetic Teacher,* 9: 134–137, March 1962.

———. "Why Not Individualized Arithmetic?" *Arithmetic Teacher,* 7: 400–403, December 1960.

Wolfson, Bernice J. "Mathematics in Multi-Age Primary Classrooms." *Wisconsin Teacher of Mathematics,* 17: June 1966.

Science

Books and Pamphlets

Elementary Science Study. *The ESS Reader.* Newton, Mass.: Education Development Center, 1970.

Howes, Virgil M. *Individualizing Instruction in Science and Mathematics: Selected Readings on Programs, Practices, and Uses of Technology.* New York: Macmillan, 1970.

McGavock, John, Jr., and Donald P. La Salle. *Guppies, Bubbles and Vibrating Objects.* New York: John Day Co., 1969.

Nuffield Foundation. *Nuffield Junior Science Project: Teachers Guides 1 and 2; Apparatus; Animals and Plants; Science and History; Autumn Into Winter; Mammals in Classrooms.* New York: John Wiley & Sons, 1967.

Magazine Articles

Cunningham, Roger. "Implementing Nongraded Advancement with Laboratory Activities As a Vehicle: An Experiment in Elementary School Science." *School Science and Mathematics,* 67: 175–181, February 1967.

Hawkins, David. "The Informed Vision: An Essay on Science Education." *Daedalus,* 94: Summer 1965.

———. "Messing About in Science." *Science and Children,* 2: February 1965.

Hedges, W. D., and M. A. MacDougall. "Teaching Fourth Grade Science by Means of Programed Science Materials with Laboratory Experiences, Phase III." *Science Education,* 49: 348–358, October 1965.

Lipson, Joseph I. "An Individualized Science Laboratory." *Science and Children,* 4: 8–12, December 1966.

Nyquist, Ewald B. "The Concept of Open Education: Its Philosophy, Historical Perspectives, and Implications." *Science Teacher,* 38: 25–28, September 1971. (This article also appears in *Education Digest,* 37: 3, 9–12, November 1971.)

Social Studies

Books

Howes, Virgil M. *Individualizing Instruction in Reading and Social Studies: Selected Readings on Programs and Practices.* New York: Macmillan, 1970.

Jones, Richard M. *Fantasy and Feeling in Education.* New York: New York University Press, 1968.

Magazine Articles

Coxe, Ross M. "Strengthening Classroom Instruction in the Social Studies." *National Elementary Principal,* 42: 30–34, May 1963.

Crabtree, Charlotte A. "Inquiry Approaches: How New and How Valuable?" *Social Education,* 30: 523–525 ff., November 1966.

"Elementary School: Focus on Individualizing Instruction." *Social Education,* 31: 405–419, May 1967. Entire issue.

Hock, Louise E. "Using Classroom Committees To Individualize Social Studies Teaching." *High School Journal,* 49: 22–29, October 1965.

Rogers, Vincent R. "Can Social Studies Be Non-Graded?" *The Instructor,* 78: 73–78, May 1969.

————. "The Individual and the Social Studies." *Social Education,* 31: 405–407 ff., May 1967.

Sloan, Fred A., Jr. "A Nongraded Social Studies Program for Grades Four, Five, and Six." *National Elementary Principal,* 45: 25–29, January 1966.

PART III: TACTICS AND STRATEGIES

Section A: Nongrading and Continuous Progress

Books and Pamphlets

Beggs, David W., III, and Edward G. Buffie, eds. *Nongraded Schools in Action: Bold New Venture.* Bloomington: Indiana University Press, 1967.

Brown, B. Frank. *The Appropriate Placement School: A Sophisticated Nongraded Curriculum.* West Nyack, New York: Parker Publishing Co., 1965.

Claremont Unified School District. *The Oakmont Nongraded Primary Program.* Claremont, Calif.: Claremont Unified School District, 1967.

Education U.S.A. Special Report. *IGE: Individually Guided Education and the Multiunit School.* Arlington, Va.: National School Public Relations Association, 1972.

Glogau, Lillian, and Murray Fessel. *The Nongraded Primary School: A Case Study.* West Nyack, New York: Parker Publishing Co., 1967.

Goodlad, John I., and Robert H. Anderson. *The Nongraded Elementary School.* Revised edition. New York: Harcourt, Brace and World, 1963.

Hillson, Maurie, and Joseph Bongo. *Continuous-Progress Education: A Practical Approach.* Chicago: Science Research Associates, 1971.

Miller, Richard I., ed. *The Nongraded School: Analysis and Study.* New York: Harper & Row, 1967.

Poway Unified School District. *Continuous Education (A Handbook for Parents).* Poway, Calif.: Poway Unified School District, 1968.

Purdom, Daniel M. *Exploring the Nongraded School.* Dayton, Ohio: Institute for Development of Educational Activities, Inc., 1970.

Rollins, Sidney P. *Developing Nongraded Schools.* Itasca, Illinois: F. E. Peacock Publishers, 1968.

Smith, Lee L. *A Practical Approach to the Nongraded Elementary School.* West Nyack, New York: Parker Publishing Company, 1968.

Tewksbury, John L. *Nongrading in the Elementary School.* Columbus, Ohio: Charles E. Merrill Books, 1967.

Winston-Salem/Forsyth County Schools. *Nongrading and Team Teaching.* Winston-Salem, N. Carolina: Winston-Salem/Forsyth County Schools, 1966.

Magazine Articles

Hillson, Maurie, ed. "The Nongraded Elementary School." *Hillson Letters.* (A series of biweekly publications, Science Research Associates, Inc., 259 E. Erie St., Chicago.) October 10, 1966, to July 3, 1967.

McLoughlin, William P. "Continuous Pupil Progress in the Non-graded School: Hope or Hoax?" *Elementary School Journal,* 71: 90–96, November 1970.

"The Nongraded School, Parts 1 and 2." *The National Elementary Principal,* 47: 2 and 3, November 1967 and January 1968.

Steere, Bob F. "Nongradedness: Relevant Research for Decision Making." *Educational Leadership,* 29: 709–711, May 1972.

Section B: School Environment and Classroom Climate

Books and Pamphlets

Abramson, Paul. *Schools for Early Childhood.* New York: Educational Facilities Laboratories, 1970.

Allen of Hurtwood, Lady. *Planning for Play.* Cambridge, Mass.: M.I.T. Press, 1969.

American Association of School Administrators. *Open Space Schools.* Washington, D.C.: the Association, 1971.

Anderson, Robert H. "The School As an Organic Teaching Aid." In *The Curriculum: Retrospect and Prospect,* 70th Yearbook, Part I. National Society for the Study of Education. Chicago: University of Chicago Press, 1971, pp. 271–306.

Association for Childhood Education International. *Learning Centers: Children on Their Own.* Washington, D.C.: the Association, 1970.

Borton, Terry. *Reach, Touch, and Teach: Student Concern and Process Education.* New York: McGraw-Hill Book Co., 1970.

Center for Urban Education. *"Open Door" New York City: A Report by the Program Reference Service.* New York: the Center, 1970.

Dennison, George. *The Lives of Children: The Story of the First Street School.* New York: Random House, 1969.

Fox, Robert S., and Ronald Lippitt. *The Human Relations School.* Ann Arbor, Michigan: Center for Research Utilization of Scientific Knowledge, University of Michigan, 1968. Mimeographed.

———— et al. *Diagnosing Classroom Learning Environments*. Chicago: Science Research Associates, 1966.

Freire, Paulo. *Pedagogy of the Oppressed*. Trans. Myra Bergman Ramos. New York: Herder and Herder, 1970.

Glasser, William. *Schools Without Failure*. New York: Harper and Row, 1969.

Glines, Don E. *Creating Humane Schools: A Guide for Implementing the Needed Revisions in the Schools & Colleges of North America*. Mankato, Minnesota: Mankato State College Campus Publishers, January 1971.

Gross, Robert, and Judith Murphy. *Educational Change and Architectural Consequences*. New York: Educational Facilities Laboratories, 1968.

Hart, Leslie A. *The Classroom Disaster*. New York: Teachers College Press, Columbia University, 1969.

Hertzberg, Alvin, and Edward F. Stone. *Schools Are for Children: An American Approach to the Open Classroom*. New York: Schocken Books, 1971.

Institute for Development of Educational Activities, Inc. *The Open Plan School*. Report of a National Seminar cosponsored by Educational Facilities Laboratories, Inc., and |I|D|E|A|. Melbourne, Florida: the Institute, 1970.

Metropolitan Toronto School Board. *Educational Specifications and User Requirements for Elementary (K–6) Schools*. Toronto, Canada: Ryerson Press, 1968.

Rasberry, Salli, and Robert Greenway. *The Rasberry Exercises: How to Start Your Own School (And Make a Book)*. Freestone, Calif.: The Freestone Publishing Co., 1970.

Richardson, Elizabeth. *The Environment of Learning*. New York: Weybright and Talley, 1967.

Rotzel, Grace. *The School in Rose Valley: A Parent Venture in Education*. Baltimore, Maryland: Johns Hopkins University Press, 1971.

Voight, Ralph C. *A Learning Center Teaching Method: Survival Kit #1*. Bethesda, Maryland: Woodmont Publishers, 1969.

Wilson, L. Craig. *The Open Access Curriculum*. Boston: Allyn and Bacon, Inc., 1971.

Magazine Articles

Audio-Visual Instruction. Vol. 12, October 1967.

Barth, Roland S. "On Selecting Materials for the Classroom." *Childhood Education,* 47: March 1971.

Pearce, Lucia. "Exploration–Innovation: The New Learning Environment." *The Science Teacher,* 36: 20–23, February 1969.

Section C: Grouping, Flexible Scheduling, and Team Teaching

Books and Pamphlets

Administrative Leadership. 5:1, February 1969. "Ability Grouping," by Cross, Passow, Hobson, and Hansen. Minneapolis, Minn.: Department of Educational Administration, College of Education, University of Minnesota, 1969.

Anderson, Robert H. "Organizing Groups for Instruction." *Individualizing Instruction.* 61st Yearbook, Part I. National Soicety for the Study of Education. Edited by Nelson B. Henry. Chicago: University of Chicago Press, 1962, pp. 239–264.

Bair, Medill, and R. G. Woodward. *Team Teaching in Action.* Boston: Houghton Mifflin Co., 1964.

Beggs, David W., III, ed. *Team Teaching: Bold New Venture.* Bloomington: Indiana University Press, 1964.

Claremont Unified School District. *An Approach to Flexible Scheduling.* Claremont, Calif.: Claremont Unified School District, 1966.

David, Harold S. *How To Organize an Effective Team Teaching Program.* Englewood Cliffs, N.J.: Prentice-Hall, 1966.

Dickinson, Marie B. *Independent and Group Learning.* Washington, D.C.: NEA Elementary Instructional Service, EKNE, n.d.

Findley, Warren G., and Miriam M. Bryan. *Ability Grouping: 1970—Status, Impact, and Alternatives.* Athens, Georgia: Center for Educational Improvement, University of Georgia, 1971.

Franklin, Marian Pope, ed. *School Organization: Theory and Practice.* Chicago: Rand McNally, 1967, Chapters 8, 9, and 10.

Franseth, Jane, and Rose Koury. *Survey of Research on Grouping As Related to Pupil Learning.* Washington, D.C.: U.S. Office of Education, 1964.

Gerard, Ralph W., ed. *Computers and Education.* New York: McGraw-Hill Book Co., 1967.

Grooms, M. Ann. *Perspectives on the Middle School.* Columbus, Ohio: Charles E. Merrill Books, 1967.

Heathers, Glen. "Guidelines for Reorganizing the School and the Classroom," in *Rational Planning in Curriculum and Instruction,* NEA, Center for the Study of Instruction, 1967, Essay Four, pp. 63–86.

Inlow, Gail M. *The Emergent in Curriculum.* New York: John Wiley & Sons, 1966, Chapter 14.

Institute for Development of Educational Activities, Inc. *Learning in the Small Group: A Classroom Manual Based on a National Seminar.* Dayton, Ohio: the Institute, 1971.

Johnson, Robert H., Jr., and John J. Hunt. *Rx for Team Teaching.* Minneapolis, Minn.: Burgess Publishing Co., 1968.

Joyce, Bruce. *The Teacher and His Staff: Man, Media and Machines.* Washington, D.C.: National Commission on Teaching Education and Professional Standards, NEA, 1967.

────── and Marsha Weil. *Models of Teaching.* Englewood Cliffs, N.J.: Prentice-Hall, 1972.

Lippitt, Peggy, Jeffrey W. Eiseman, and Ronald Lippitt. *Cross-Age Helping Program: Dissemination Materials.* 2 vols. Ann Arbor, Michigan: Center for Research on Utilization of Scientific Knowledge, Institute for Social Research, University of Michigan, 1968. Program includes filmstrip, two records, script, and directions.

Lobb, Delbert M. *Practical Aspects of Team Teaching.* Palo Alto, California: Fearon Publishers, Inc., 1964.

Morgenstern, Anne, ed. *Grouping in the Elementary School.* New York: Pitman Publishing Corp., 1966.

National Education Association. Department of Elementary-Kindergarten-Nursery Education. *Multi-Age Grouping: Enriching the Learning Environment.* Washington, D.C.: National Education Association, 1968.

──────, Research Division. "Ability Grouping." Research Summary, 1968–S3. Washington, D.C.: NEA Research Division, 1968.

Norwalk, Connecticut Board of Education. *The Norwalk Plan of Team Teaching: Fifth Report.* Norwalk, Connecticut: Norwalk Board of Education, 1962–63.

Ontario-Monclair School District, California. *A Cross-Age Teaching Resource Manual.* John Mainiero, Coordinator. Ontario, California: Ontario-Monclair School District, 1971.

Petrequin, Gaynor. *Individualizing Learning Through Modular-Flexible Programming.* New York: McGraw-Hill Book Co., 1968.

Polos, Nicholas C. *The Dynamics of Team Teaching.* Dubuque, Iowa: William C. Brown Co., 1965.

Ridgway, Lorna. *Family Grouping in the Primary School.* New York: Agathon Press, 1971.

Shaplin, Judson T., and H. F. Olds, eds. *Team Teaching.* New York: Harper & Row, 1964.

Thelen, Herbert A., et al. *Classroom Grouping for Teachability.* Chicago: University of Chicago, 1967. (See annotation in Part I.)

Trump, J. Lloyd, and D. F. Miller. "Team Teaching and Improved Staff Utilization." *Secondary School Curriculum Improvement: Proposals and Procedures.* Boston: Allyn and Bacon, 1968.

Tyler, C. Edward. *Team Teaching.* Curriculum Bulletin, no. 286. Eugene, Oregon: School of Education, University of Oregon, 1968.

Westby-Gibson, Dorothy. *Grouping Students for Improved Instruction.* Englewood Cliffs, N.J.: Prentice-Hall, 1966.

Wisconsin Improvement Program. *Experiences in Team Teaching.* Madison: School of Education, University of Wisconsin, 1963.

Yates, Alfred, ed. *Grouping in Education*. New York: John Wiley & Sons, 1966.

York, L. Jean. *Teaching Modules on Team Teaching*. 7 vols. Austin, Texas: Research and Development Center for Teacher Education, University of Texas, 1969–70.

Magazine Articles

Carruth, Harold, and R. P. Hichborn. "Trying Team Teaching in Science." *Science Teacher*, 32: 29–30, November 1965.

Fischler, Abraham S., and Peter B. Shoresman. "Team Teaching in the Elementary School: Implications for Research in Science Instruction." *Science Education*, 46: 406–415, December 1962.

Gaskell, William, and Jack Sheridan. "Team Teaching and the Social Studies in the Elementary School." *Elementary School Journal*, 68: 246–250, February 1968.

Section D: Computer-Assisted and Programmed Instruction

Books and Pamphlets

American Association of Elementary-Kindergarten-Nursery Education, NEA. *Elementary School Media Programs: An Approach to Individualizing Instruction*. Washington, D.C.: National Education Association Center, 1970.

American Association of School Administrators. *Instructional Technology and the School Administrator*. Prepared by the AASA Committee on Technology and Instruction. Edited by Stephen J. Knezevich and Glen G. Eye. Washington, D.C., 1970.

Bushnell, Donald D., and Dwight W. Allen, eds. *The Computer in American Education*. New York: John Wiley & Sons, 1967.

Computers: New Era for Education? Education U.S.A. Special Report. Washington, D.C.: National School Public Relations Association, 1968.

Cooley, William W., and Robert Glaser. *An Information and Management System for Individually Prescribed Instruction*. Working Paper 44. Pittsburgh: Learning Research and Development Center, University of Pittsburgh, 1968.

Education U.S.A. Special Report. *Computers: New Era for Education?* Washington, D.C.: National School Public Relations Association, 1968.

————. *Individually Prescribed Instruction*. Washington, D.C.: Education U.S.A., 1968.

Esbenson, Thorwald. *Working with Individualized Instruction*. San Francisco: Fearon Publishers, 1968.

Gerard, Ralph W., ed. *Computers and Education*. New York: McGraw-Hill Book Co., 1967.

Glaser, Robert. "The Design of Instruction." *The Changing American School*. 65th Yearbook, Part II. National Society for the Study of Education, edited by John I. Goodlad. Chicago: University of Chicago Press, 1966, pp. 215–242.

————, ed. *Teaching Machines and Programmed Learning, II: Data and Directions*. Washington, D.C.: National Education Association, 1965.

———— et al. *Studies of the Use of Programmed Instruction in the Intact Classroom*. Pittsburgh: Learning Research and Development Center, University of Pittsburgh, 1963.

Goodlad, John I. *The Future of Learning and Teaching* (Address at the NEA inauguration of Dr. Sam Lambert). Washington, D.C.: NEA, 1968.

————, et al. *Computers and Information Systems in Education*. New York: Harcourt, Brace and World, 1966.

Institute for Development of Educational Activities. *The Computer in Education*. Melbourne, Fla.: the Institute, 1970.

Jackson, Philip W. *The Teacher and the Machine* (Horace Mann Lecture, 1967). Pittsburgh, Pa.: The University of Pittsburgh, 1968.

Jacobs, Paul I., et al. *A Guide to Evaluating Self-Instructional Programs*. New York: Holt, Rinehart and Winston, Inc., 1966.

Johnson, M. Clemens. *Educational Uses of the Computer: An Introduction*. Chicago: Rand McNally & Co., 1971.

Joyce, Bruce R. *The Teacher and His Staff: Man, Media and Machines*. Washington, D.C.: National Education Association, 1967.

Lindvall, C. M., and John O. Bolvin. "Programmed Instruction in the Schools: An Application of Programming Principles in Individually Prescribed Instruction." *Programmed Instruction*. 66th Yearbook, Part II, National Society for the Study of Education, edited by Phil C. Lange. Chicago: University of Chicago Press, 1967, pp. 217–254.

Molnar, Andres R., and Beverly Sherman. *U.S. Office of Education Support of Computer Activities*. Washington, D.C.: U.S. Office of Education, 1969.

Oettinger, Anthony C. *Run, Computer, Run: The Mythology of Educational Innovation*. Cambridge, Mass.: Harvard University Press, 1969.

Skinner, B. F. *The Technology of Teaching*. New York: Appleton-Century-Crofts, 1968.

Suppes, Patrick. *Computer-Assisted Instruction in the Schools: Potentialities, Problems, Prospects*. (Institute for Mathematical Studies in the Social Sciences, Technical Reports, No. 81.) Stanford, Calif.: Stanford University Press, 1965.

U.S. Congress, House Committee on Education and Labor. *To Improve Learning*. A Report to the President and the Congress by the Commission on Instructional Technology. Washington, D.C.: U.S. Government Printing Office, March 1970.

Weisgerber, Robert A., ed. *Instructional Process and Media Innovation*. Chicago: Rand McNally, 1968.

Magazine Articles

Atkinson, Richard C., and D. N. Hansen. "Computer-Assisted Instruction in Initial Reading: The Stanford Project." *Reading Research Quarterly*, 2: 5–25, Fall 1966.

Bolvin, John O., and Robert Glaser. "Developmental Aspects of Individually Prescribed Instruction." *Audio Visual Instruction*, 13: 829 ff., October 1968.

Campbell, Vincent N. "Research on Self-Directed Learning in the Classroom." *Programmed Instruction*, 4: 1–2, November 1964.

Carlson, Elliot. "Education and Industry: Troubled Partnership." *Saturday Review*, August 15, 1970, pp. 45–47, 58–60.

Cogswell, John F. "Humanistic Approaches to the Design of Schools." In A. M. Kroll, ed. *Issues in American Education: Commentary on the Current Scene*. New York: Oxford University Press, 1970, pp. 98–117.

Coulson, John E. "Automation, Electronic Computers, and Education." *Phi Delta Kappan*, 47: 340–344, March 1966 .

Filep, Robert. "Individualized Instruction and the Computer: Potential for Mass Education." *A-V Communication Review*, 15: 102–112, Spring 1967.

Flanagan, John C. "Functional Education for the Seventies." *Phi Delta Kappan*, 49: 27–32, September 1967.

Florida Educational Research and Development Council. "Research and the Teacher: Ability Grouping." *Research Bulletin*, 1: August 1965.

Gentile, J. Ronald. "The First Generation of Computer-Assisted Instructional Systems: An Evaluation Review." *A-V Communication Review*, 15: 23–58, Spring 1967.

Gold, Milton J. "Focusing on Teaching Needs." *Educational Leadership*, 20: 434–437, 458, April 1963.

Gray, Genevieve. "Educational Technology and the Individual Student." *Phi Delta Kappan*, 46: 6–8, September 1964.

Gropper, George L., and G. C. Kress. "Individualizing Instruction through Pacing Procedures." *A-V Communication Review*, 13: 165–182, Summer 1965.

Gurau, Peter K. "Data Processing in a Continuous Progress Program." *Educational Technology*, 8: 5–12, May 15, 1968.

Mager, Robert F. "Learner-Controlled Instruction—1958–1964." *Programmed Instruction*, Vol. 4, November 1964.

Oettinger, Anthony G. "The Myths of Educational Technology." *Saturday Review*, 51: 76–77 ff., May 18, 1968.

Suppes, Patrick. "The Computer and Excellence." *Saturday Review*, 50: 46–50, January 14, 1967.

Zinn, Karl L. "Computer Technology for Teaching and Research on Instruction." *Review of Educational Research*, 37: 618–634, December 1967.

PART IV: FILMS

Charlie and the Golden Hamster—The Nongraded Elementary School. 13 min., 16 mm, color. |I|D|E|A|, Box 446, Melbourne, Florida 32901.

Children As People: The Fayerweather Street School. 35 min., 16 mm, black and white.
John Holt narrates film of this private school in Cambridge, Mass., run on principles similar to British primary schools. Polymorph Films, Inc., Boston, Mass.

Choosing To Learn. 26 min., 16 mm, color.
An Elementary Science Study film showing the World of Inquiry School in Rochester, New York, where children choose their own activities. Education Development Center, Inc., Newton, Mass. 02160.

Discovery and Experience. 10 films, 30 min. each, 16 mm, black and white.
The child's need for exploration and self-discovery are stressed in this BBC-TV series. Available in the U.S. through Time-Life Films, Rockefeller Center, New York, N.Y. 10020.

How To Provide Personalized Education in a Public School. 16 mm, black and white.
A series of five filmed lectures on individualizing instruction available from Special Purpose Films, 26740 Latigo Shore Drive, Malibu, California 90265.
Can Individualization Work in Your School System?
Part I. 41 min. John I. Goodlad, narrator.
How Can You Make Individualization Work in Your School System?
Part II. 35 min. Madeline Hunter, narrator.
Why Are Team Teaching and Nongrading Important?
Part III. 49 min. John I. Goodlad, narrator.
How Can You Apply Team Teaching and Nongrading to Your School?
Part IV. 35 min. Madeline Hunter, narrator.
How Can the Curriculum for Individualized Education Be Determined?
Part V. 35 min. John I. Goodlad, narrator.

I Am Here Today. 43 min., 16 mm, black and white.

A companion piece to Betsye Sargent's report, *The Integrated Day in an American School* (see listing in Part I). Education Development Center, Inc., Newton, Mass. 02160.

Infants School. 32 min., 16 mm, black and white.

Filmed and narrated by visiting educator, Lillian Weber, at the Gordonbrock Infant School focusing on children's movement in the classroom. Unedited. Education Development Center, Inc., Newton, Mass. 02160.

The League. 16 mm, black and white.

A series of four film reports and three excerpts from the documentaries on |I|D|E|A|'s Study of Educational Change and School Improvement (SECSI). Distributed by |I|D|E|A|, Box 446, Melbourne, Florida 32901.

The Strategy.

Part I. 60 min.

A Matter of Trust.

Part II. 28 min.

Try It Sometime.

Part III. 40 min.

I Just Wanted To Let You Know How Well Rhonda Is Doing in School.

Part IV. 35 min.

Case History of a Teaching Team.

Excerpt. 25 min.

Staff Meeting.

Excerpt. 10 min. Shows staff discussion of problems involved in individualizing.

Why Visit Another School.

Excerpt. 15 min. Teachers visit a highly individualized classroom and discuss pros and cons with staff upon return.

Let Them Learn. 27 min., 16 mm, color.

The story of *Project Discovery* produced by Encyclopaedia Britannica Educational Corporation, Public Relations Dept., 425 N. Michigan Ave., Chicago, Ill. 60611.

Make a Mighty Reach. 45 min., 16 mm, color.

Depicts innovation in schools throughout the U.S. Distributed by |I|D|E|A|, Box 446, Melbourne, Florida 32901.

More Different Than Alike. 35 min., 16 mm, color.

Shows schools in initial attempts to individualize instruction. National Education Association, National Commission on Teacher Education and Professional Standards, 1201 Sixteenth St., N.W., Washington, D.C. 20036.

My Name Is Children. 60 min., 16 mm, black and white.

A National Educational Television presentation. Indiana University, Bloomington, Indiana 47401.

Primary Education in England: The English Infant School. 17 min., 16 mm, color.
   Depicts the Sea Mills Infant School in Bristol, England. Institute for Development of Educational Activities, Inc., Information and Services Division, Box 446, Melbourne, Florida 32901.

Project Plan. 30 min., 16 mm, black and white.
   Presents the viewpoints of the Program for Learning in Accordance with Needs (PLAN) founder, Dr. John C. Flanagan, and his associates at the American Institutes for Research, Palo Alto, California. Far West Laboratory for Educational Research and Development, 1 Garden Circle, Hotel Claremont, Berkeley, California 94705.

The Quiet Revolution. 28 min., 16 mm, color.
   Concerns teacher aids and other reforms. National Education Association, National Commission on Teacher Education and Professional Standards, 1201 Sixteenth St., N.W., Washington, D.C. 20036.

The Summer Children. 44 min., 16 mm, color.
   The story of a summer program for a group of four- to eight-year-old disadvantaged children at the University Elementary School, University of California at Los Angeles. Academic Communications Facility, University of California at Los Angeles, Los Angeles, California 90024.

Teaching the One and the Many. 28 min., 16 mm, color.
   National Education Association, National Commission on Teacher Education and Professional Standards, 1201 Sixteenth St., N.W., Washington, D.C. 20036.

Team Teaching in the Elementary Level. 14 min., 16 mm, color.
   Experiment in Cashmere, Washington, portraying the purpose and methodology of team teaching. Bailey Films, 6509 De Longpre Ave., Hollywood, California 90029.

Team Teaching in the Elementary School. 17 min., 16 mm, color.
   Designed as in-service training film for educators already committed to teaching teams. |I|D|E|A|, Box 446, Melbourne, Florida 32901.

They Can Do It. 34 min., 16 mm, black and white.
   Shows first grade taught by Lovey Glen in Philadelphia as she moves the class from a traditional to a more open structure. Education Development Center, Inc., Newton, Mass. 02160.

PART V: AUDIO TAPES

Anderson, Robert H., and Evelyn M. Carswell. *The Nongraded School: Some Questions and Comments.* National Education Association, Washington, D.C., 1968.

Bailey, Stephen K. *Education and the Pursuit of Happiness.* The Sir John Adams Lecture, UCLA, April 28, 1971.

Broudy, Harry S. *Stress and Distress in the School As a Social System.* 24th ASCD Annual Conference, 1969.

Combs, Arthur W. *Humanizing Education: The Person in the Process.* 22nd ASCD Conference, Dallas, 1967.

Deterline, William. "Individualized Instruction," in *Sound Education Reports,* 1:11, 1970.

Fisher, Duke. *The Turned-On Generation.* California Association for Supervision and Curriculum Development, Fresno, California, 1968.

Frymier, Jack. *Rebellion: Today's Dilemma.* California Association for Supervision and Curriculum Development, Fresno, California, 1968.

Goodlad, John I. *Planning and Organizing for Teaching.* NEA, Washington, D.C., 1964.

————. *Speaking of Individualization.* Educational Resource Associates, Inc., 1973.

————. *Speaking of Nongrading.* Educational Resource Associates, Inc., 1973.

————. *Speaking of Team Teaching.* Educational Resource Associates, Inc., 1973.

Illich, Ivan. *Comments.* AERA Annual Meeting, 1971.

Michael, Donald, and Sidney M. Jourard. *Actualization and Alienation.* 22nd Association for Supervisors and Curriculum Development Conference, Dallas, Texas, 1967.

National Education Association. *Schools for the '70's.* Discussion-Starter Tape Library Cassettes. National Education Association, Center for the Study of Instruction, Washington, D.C., 1971.

Rogers, Carl R. *The Interpersonal Relationship in Learning.* 22nd Association for Supervision and Curriculum Development Conference, Dallas, Texas, 1967.

Sand, Ole. *Talks with Teachers. Schools for the '70's* series. National Education Association, Center for the Study of Instruction, 1971.